新航道 NEW CHANNEL

# 9 分达人

新航道雅思研发中心
[英]詹姆斯(James Foster) ◎ 编著

# 雅思写作宝典

2019—2023年雅思写作 **新题** + **4套** 全真模拟题

☑ 考官视角解读评分标准 剖析得分要点
☑ 教学视角精析外教范文 学习地道表达
☑ 解密写作思路 助力考生领悟解题精髓

**2023.4**
Hosting major international
sporting events

**2023.2**
Pay for healthcare
and education

**2021.8**
Local library
(table)

**2020.9**
ore adults will
k from home

**2021.7**
The participation in
organised cultural activities
and sports (bar chart)

**2020.3**
The news has no
connection with most
people's lives

**2020.6**
The temperature and
hours of daylight in two
different cities (table)

**2023.1**
Some ex-prisoners
commit crimes

**2020.8**
Social networking sites

全新真题

世界知识出版社

**图书在版编目（CIP）数据**

9分达人雅思写作宝典 / 新航道雅思研发中心，（英）詹姆斯（James Foster）编著 . -- 北京：世界知识出版社，2023.11
ISBN 978-7-5012-6692-0

Ⅰ.①9… Ⅱ.①新… ②詹… Ⅲ.① IELTS －写作－自学参考资料 Ⅳ.① H315

中国国家版本馆 CIP 数据核字（2023）第 196044 号

| | |
|---|---|
| 责任编辑 | 谢　晴 |
| 特约编辑 | 龚玲琳 |
| 特邀编辑 | 王丽娜　商　文　赵　博 |
| 责任出版 | 赵　玥 |
| 责任校对 | 张　琨 |
| 书　　名 | **9分达人雅思写作宝典**<br>9 Fen Daren Yasi Xiezuo Baodian |
| 编　　著 | 新航道雅思研发中心　　［英］詹姆斯（James Foster） |
| 出版发行 | 世界知识出版社 |
| 地址邮编 | 北京市东城区干面胡同 51 号（100010） |
| 网　　址 | www.ishizhi.cn |
| 电　　话 | 010-65233645（市场部） |
| 经　　销 | 新华书店 |
| 印　　刷 | 清淞永业（天津）印刷有限公司 |
| 开本印张 | 787 毫米×1092 毫米　1/16　12 1/4 印张 |
| 字　　数 | 279 千字 |
| 版次印次 | 2023 年 11 月第 1 版　2023 年 11 月第 1 次印刷 |
| 标准书号 | ISBN 978-7-5012-6692-0 |
| 定　　价 | 59.00 元 |

**Congratulations on taking a step forward to achieving an improved IELTS Writing score!**

**恭喜你，在提高雅思写作成绩之路上又迈进了一步！**

Firstly, some figures. According to the IELTS Test Taker Performance statistics in 2022, the Academic Mean Performance of Chinese Candidates for Writing was less than 6; 5.8, to be precise. (You can find this information here – https://www.ielts.org/for-researchers/test-statistics/test-taker-performance.) However, an IELTS score of 6.5, 7.0 or maybe even higher is required to study at a highly-ranked university in the UK. This is the primary reason for this book – to help students improve their IELTS exam score to obtain the conditions of a university offer successfully, not just in the UK but in other countries too, as the IELTS Test is recognised worldwide.

首先分享几个数据。根据 "2022年雅思考生成绩表现" 统计，中国考生的学术类写作平均成绩不到6分，更精确地说是5.8分。（具体信息见 https://www.ielts.org/for-researchers/test-statistics/test-taker-performance。）然而，如果要就读英国排名靠前的大学，雅思总分需达到6.5分、7分甚至更高。由于雅思考试在全球范围内被认可，本书旨在帮助学生提高雅思成绩，以达到英国或其他国家大学的语言入学条件。

I have designed this book, as part of the "9分达人" series, to help IELTS candidates know and fully understand what the examiners are looking for when assessing candidates after the exam, namely the IELTS Writing criteria. I will describe, in detail, the reasons for some of the administration and the two tasks of the Academic and General exams: Task 1 and Task 2. I will also go through several example answers using real questions, comment and give tips, advice and useful phrases that can be used.

作为 "9分达人" 系列之一，本书列出了雅思写作评分标准，帮助考生充分理解考官在评估雅思作文时的评分思路。我将详细描述一些评分依据和学术类/培训类写作考试的两个部分：Task 1和 Task 2。我还会以真题为例，提供范文示例和评论，并列出相应的提示、建议和有用的短语。

I firmly believe that using the knowledge of the criteria can help you on the path to passing the IELTS exam at your required level. It should be understood that this is NOT a 'quick fix' book, but one that can point you in the right direction to improve.

我坚信了解写作评分标准会帮助你通过雅思写作考试并取得预期分数。然而有一点要清楚，这不是一本 "快速通关" 指南，但却会为你指明改进提升的正确方向。

## ■ Some Details about the Exam Procedure 考试流程细节

The Writing exam is typically taken on the same day as the Listening and Reading exams, so expect a long morning or afternoon, as all three of them will take you over two and a half hours. The timing of the General writing exam is the same as the Academic one; you will have 60 minutes for both and will be given paper and a pencil to use. At the time of writing this book, in mid-2023, more and more of the exams are being conducted online. If you book one of these, you will obviously need to type your answer rather than write them, so my first tip would be to practice your typing for both accuracy and speed, as you still will only have an hour to complete the exam.

写作考试通常与听力和阅读考试在同一天进行，所以要准备好度过一个漫长的上午或下午，因为这三项考试加起来超过两个半小时。培训类写作考试和学术类时长一样，你需要在60分钟内完成写作，试卷与铅笔会当场发给你。在写本书期间，即2023年中，越来越多的考试在线上进行。如果你报名了机考，很显然你不需要手写，而是在键盘上敲出答案。所以我的第一个建议是练习打字的准确性和速度，因为你仍然只有一个小时完成写作考试。

## ■ The Examination Structure 写作考试结构

### ▶ Academic and General 学术类与培训类

The Writing section has two types: Academic and General. For those wishing to study in the UK or elsewhere, you must take the Academic version. If you are purely going to visit or immigrate, you can do the General version. My advice, though, is whatever you're trying to do, the Academic version will probably be more helpful.

雅思写作考试有两种类型：学术类与培训类。对于那些希望在英国或其他地方学习的人，你必须参加学术类考试；如果你纯粹是去旅游或移民，你可以参加培训类考试。不过，我的建议是，不论你的目的是什么，学术类考试可能会更有帮助。

> **Task 1**　A Graph, Table, Map or Process (Academic) 图表题、表格题、地图题与流程图题 ( 学术类 )

In Task 1 of the Writing exam, you are given a graph, table, map or process where you are asked to describe or summarise the information in a minimum of 150 words.

写作考试的 Task 1通常有四种题型：图表题、表格题、地图题或流程图题，你需要根据提示用至少150字来描述或总结信息。

Generally, with a graph or table, you'll need to summarise the data; with a process, you'll need to explain the different stages; and with a map, you'll need to describe it.

通常，图表题与表格题需要你总结数据，流程图题需要你对不同阶段做解释，地图题需要你对地图进行描述。

## Task 1    A Letter (General) 书信（培训类）

In Task 1 of the General exam, you are required to write a letter. It can be in one of three forms: Informal, Semi-formal, or Formal and can be one of many different types. For example, it can be a letter of Appreciation, Invitation, Suggestion etc., and just like the Academic version, it should be at least 150 words. The instructions are typically as follows:

培训类考试的 Task 1的要求是写一封信。有以下3种形式：非正式、半正式与正式，可能涉及很多不同的类型。例如，可能会是一封感谢信、邀请信或者建议书等。和学术类考试一样，字数要求为最少150字。题目格式通常如下：

To whom you are writing and the reason for the letter.

列出写信的对象和原因。

Details in your letter

• Detail 1

• Detail 2

• Detail 3

在信中，你需要列出3项内容。

Write at least 150 words. You do NOT need to write any addresses.

字数要求至少150字。你不需要写地址。

Begin your letter as follows:

信的开头参考如下：

Dear ...,

It's essential that you open and close the letter properly, as well as have the appropriate structure. Details about these are covered in the Task 1 – General, Approach section a little later in this book.

在信中恰当地开头与结尾很重要，同样重要的是行文结构要合理。在本书稍后的章节，会对 Task 1 的写法作详细介绍。

## Task 2    An Argumentative/Exemplification Essay 议论型／例证型作文

With Task 2, there are a few different types of questions, but what does remain consistent is the following:

在 Task 2中，有一些不同类型的问题，但下面这个部分在每个题型中都保持一致：

**Give reasons for your answer and include any relevant examples from your own knowledge or experience. Write at least 250 words.**

The types of questions you can come across are: to agree or disagree with a point of view or argument, discuss two opposing views, the advantages or disadvantages of a given topic, explain a given problem, or lastly, the cause of a problem and offer a solution.

常见的题型如下：同意或不同意某种观点或争议，讨论两个截然相反的观点，所给话题的利弊，解释一个问题，以及分析某个问题产生的原因并给出解决策略。

A little later in this book, I will go through each of these in detail so you can properly understand how to approach them.

在本书的稍后部分，我会详细介绍上述题型，帮助你正确理解如何处理这些题型。

*Important Tip:* *Task 2's score is worth around twice that of Task 1, so I strongly suggest you do Task 2 first. If you do this and don't finish Task 1, you'll lose fewer marks than if you do it the other way around.*

**重要提示：** Task 2 的分值是 Task 1 的两倍。因此，我强烈建议你在考试中先写 Task 2。这样，即使你最后没有完成 Task 1，你丢掉的分数也会比反过来做少。

## ■ The Band Scores 分数等级

There is no pass or fail in the IELTS Exam, simply different levels or 'Band Scores' as they are officially known. The table below shows the nine different levels of IELTS. I have also added TOEFL iBT and CEFR system so you can easily compare them. Some scores don't match each other exactly, so use this as a rough guide.

雅思考试没有及格或不及格的说法，只有不同的水平或官方的"分数等级"。下表显示了雅思考试的 9 个不同级别。我还添加了托福网考和欧洲语言共同参考框架（Common European Framework of Reference for Languages，简称 CEFR）以方便比较。有些分数与等级之间并不完全匹配，因此仅供粗略参考。

| IELTS Score | TOEFL iBT | CEFR |
|---|---|---|
| 9 – Expert User | 118 | C2 |
| 8 – Very Good User | 110 | C1 |
| 7 – Good User | 94 | |
| 6 – Competent User | 60 | B2 |
| 5 – Modest User | 35 | B1 |
| 4 – Limited User | | A2 |
| 3 – Extremely Limited User | 0 - 31 | A1 |
| 2 – Intermittent User | | |
| 1 – Non User | | |

Often, candidates will receive half marks (5.5 or 6.5, for example). This is because the overall score is the calculated mean average from the individual scores of each exam element. See below for an example:

通常，考生的分数会出现半分的情况（例如 5.5 或 6.5）。这是因为总分是根据每个单项分数计算出的平均分。请参见下例：

| Listening | Reading | Writing | Speaking | Overall |
|-----------|---------|---------|----------|---------|
| 7 | 6 | 6 | 6.5 | 6.5 |

*Tiny Tip:* *Individual Element Scores are rounded down, whereas, to balance things, Overall scores are rounded up.*

小提示：单项分数向下取整，为了平衡，总分向上取整。

## ■ ChatGPT and Other Chatbots ChatGPT 及其他聊天机器人

A recent technological development is that of AI, particularly ChatGPT. At the time of writing, mid 2023, it has been all over the news and Internet for weeks, and many people are unsure how it can, or will be, incorporated into learning and education.

最近的技术进展当属人工智能，特别是 ChatGPT。本书撰写时正值 2023 年中，它连续数周出现在新闻和互联网上，许多人还不确定能否或者如何将其应用于学习和教育中。

Many teachers and universities have already raised the questions of plagiarism and copyright, and, to my knowledge, there aren't any definite answers at the moment. Having looked at, and used it, a little myself, I would have to say that if you just copy/memorise the answers given for the IELTS writing exam, it will be self-evident.

许多老师和大学已经提出了剽窃和版权的问题，并且据我所知，目前还没有任何明确的解决方案。我自己了解并尝试了一下，不得不说，如果你全部复制或记忆它提供的雅思写作考试答案，考官能明显看出是机器生成的。

I say this for two reasons. The first is that the answers are given in a very formal format, and the second is that the structures of the answers are always the same, quite often with the same vocabulary being used.

我这样说有两个原因：第一，答案过于正式；第二，所有答案的结构几乎一致，相同的词汇也经常重复使用。

I realise that some technology companies have now brought out their own versions, and I wish them luck, but DON'T use them to give you answers that you can memorise. It's possible that you could get away with it once, or even more than that, but if you think about this logically, it will be that there are thousands of people doing exactly the same and producing VERY similar answers, so if an examiner reads the same response from multiple students, they are likely to raise questions and report candidates to the administration team.

我知道一些科技公司都将在不久的将来推出自己的版本，我祝他们好运，但请不要使用人工智能给你提供能记住的答案。你可能会侥幸成功一次，甚至更多次，但如果你从逻辑上思考这个问题，会发现有成千上万的人在做完全相同的事情，并给出非常相似的答案。如果考官读到多个学生的回答相同，他们很可能会提出质疑，将考生情况报告给管理团队。

I would advise using them to give you ideas and maybe even facts and then using your knowledge and language to describe those ideas. This will not only help you improve your English but also help you understand how to improve your grammar and idea development.

我的建议是仅让它们提供想法或者一些实例，然后用你的知识和语言来描述这些想法。这不仅能帮助你提高英语水平，还能帮助你理解如何提升语法和思路拓展。

## ■ Some "Thank yous" 致谢

Before I get into the examples and descriptions, I'd like to thank some people who helped make this book a reality.

进入正文之前，我想感谢以下这些人，他们的帮助使这本书顺利出版。

Cindy Ge, from New Channel, her constant advice and support were invaluable in keeping me motivated during this content's design and actual writing. Shelley Du, from New Channel, who helped with the content design and supplied me with more than enough questions to complete this first edition. Ms. Zhao Bo, from New Channel, for their meticulous care, intriguing ideas and questions. Rena Wang, from New Channel, for her patience with my constant questions. I'm sure that without their help and the rest of the New Channel team, this would at least be a very different book and, at worst, not a book at all.

新航道的葛亚芬老师持续给予我宝贵的建议与支持，是我构思和创作的动力来源；杜修丽老师帮我构思内容，为我提供丰富的真题以完成本书第一版；感谢赵博老师给予这本书无微不至的关怀、有趣的想法和问题，以及王丽娜老师对我不断提出的问题的耐心。我敢肯定，如果没有他们和新航道其他成员的帮助，这本书会截然不同，甚至难以成形。

詹姆斯

2023 年 8 月

新航道"9分达人"系列图书已面世十余载,陪伴雅思考生走过了许多备考的日日夜夜。雅思写作分册迄今共出版了四册,五年磨一剑,在 **2023** 年,本系列迎来了全新的版本。这本《**9**分达人雅思写作宝典》选取 **2019–2023** 年雅思写作全新真题,第一次从考官的角度对评分标准进行了具体的阐述。希望在全新的视角和学习方式的助力下,考生能够精准备考,提高考试成绩和写作能力。

本书由新航道雅思研发中心与詹姆斯(James Foster)共同创作出版,目的是打造一本"明确考官想要的,提供考生要学的"书。詹姆斯在英语教学的各个方面都有着丰富的经验。作为一名前雅思考官,他先后在北京多所大学工作,已有 **15** 年的在华教学经验,对中国学生的需求有着独特的见解。有感于中国学生在英语学习和雅思考试通过方面所面临的困难,他非常期待通过本书,为考生提供帮助。以下是本书在编排上的几个特色。

**1. 考官视角解读评分标准　剖析得分要点**

如今,市场上雅思写作方面的参考用书大体分为两类。其一,作者像上课一样洋洋洒洒地将自己对于雅思写作的所有理解分章节地写出来,事无巨细,从字、词、句、语法等各个环节手把手教导,而这类书往往写作角度比较单一,内容比较主观。其二,就是范文书,主要是呈现所谓的高分范文,并配有简要讲解。

然而,本书另辟蹊径,从剑桥雅思官方的 Task Achievement(Task 1)& Task Response(Task 2)(任务完成及任务回应)、Cohesion and Coherence(衔接和连贯)、Lexical Resource(词汇多样性)和 Grammatical Range and Accuracy(语法多样性和准确性)四大评分标准出发,通过中英文对照的方式让考生直接了解雅思写作考官在评分时的依据,逐条分析并举例说明,将评分标准中"基本的""不足""有效地""恰当地"等表达具象化,向考生更好地阐明在雅思考试过程中,考官到底看重什么,从而让考生在写作文时尽量按照评分标准中设置的具体要求来写,避免扣分点。不仅如此,作者针对中国考生的语言和思路的弱点,还逐步展示了从 **4** 分到 **7** 分四大标准的不同例子,让考生能更好地了解自己的水平以及进步空间,从而更有针对性地进行备考。

**2. 教学视角精析外教范文　学习地道表达**

作为前雅思考官,詹姆斯多年的任教经验让他在编写写作范文时,能充分了解考生日常会踩的"坑",并巧妙地融合到答案范例和评析建议中去,让学生看到就能产生"是我了"的熟悉感,从而绕道而行。

为了向考生提供更加精准的备考建议，本书在 Section Ⅱ 中提供了写作 Task 1 中会遇到的 5 种题目类型（学术类有 4 种，培训类有 1 种）及其 17 篇原汁原味的外教范文，其中流畅地道的表达，清晰的逻辑，并配上地道的翻译，对考生大有裨益。每篇范文的考官评析，都从 3 大方面——Coherence and Cohesion（衔接和连贯）、Lexical Resource（词汇多样性）以及 Grammatical Range and Accuracy（语法多样性和准确性）进行点评，接着又细化为 6 个维度，分别为：Logical（逻辑）、Progression（推进）、Range（词汇多样性）、Less Common（不常用词汇）、Simple Structures（简单句）以及 Complex Structures（复杂句）。每个维度不仅给出该维度达成与否的标识，而且在推进、词汇多样性和不常用词汇维度方面，从范文中摘出相关的短语和词汇，让考生明白哪些表达可以让作文更加分，从而进一步丰富考生的写作词库。

书中题目都极具代表性、针对性和指导性。雅思写作的学习与练习题目并不在多，而在精。真题浩瀚，不能穷尽。在 Section Ⅲ 中，本书提供了写作 Task 2 的双边讨论类型、同意与否类型、积极消极讨论类型和其他混合提问类型的 4 种题目类型和精心准备的 30 篇外教答案范例。该部分同样在推进、词汇多样性和不常用词汇这 3 个维度从范文中摘出相关的短语和词汇，让考生明白打造高分作文的"密码"，帮助考生了解雅思写作考官喜欢的文章写法以及适合雅思写作的语言和思路特点。

### 3. 解密写作思路　助力考生领悟解题精髓

一篇作文想要出彩，首先需要良好的构思，本书每篇范文都给出了"思考"的过程。在 Section Ⅱ 中，由表及里，用清晰简洁的语言为考生精准提炼出每篇作文的题目类型，并梳理出作文主体段的"脉络"，让考生快速明白每篇作文的框架结构和行文思路，也对自己今后遇到不同题目类型的写作思路处理有了针对性的指导。让考生在考场拿到题目的时候，能灵活运用本书中所学到的写作方法，快速分析出以下几个问题：（1）这是什么题目类型；（2）主体段需要写几段；（3）每段主体段需要安排什么内容。从而快速进行谋篇布局，缩短前期的思考时间，为后面的行文留出更多的时间去进行遣词造句。

Section Ⅲ，与 Section Ⅱ 略有不同，此部分呈现了每篇作文的"题目关键词"和"构思"，让考生先学会第一步正确审题，再去有效"解题"。

考试的准备并非一朝一夕的事情，写作的进步除了仔细了解考试评分标准和参考范文，更重要的是明白写作的根本是不断的思考与积累。希望本书能够架起考官与考生之间的桥梁，传达考官所需要的，给予考生所要学的，能助力考生通过孜孜不倦的积累与日复一日的训练，成为在考场上文思泉涌的那个闪亮的人。感谢本书作者詹姆斯将多年的心得一字一句地写出并传授给考生，也感谢新航道雅思研发中心每一位为本书辛勤付出的老师们。欢迎各位读者朋友们提出宝贵意见与建议，共同翻越语言的障碍，更流畅地与世界对话！

最后需要说明的是，作者詹姆斯来自英国，所有范文均由他撰写，仅代表其个人观点。

# CONTENTS
目　　　录

## Section II  Task 1 Preparation and Question Types　Task 1 备考及问题类型

## Section III  Task 2 Preparation and Question Types　Task 2 备考及问题类型

## 附录 Module Tests and Sample Answers  真题模拟及参考答案

# Section I

## The IELTS Writing Criteria

### 雅思写作评分标准

I believe that understanding the IELTS Writing Criteria is fundamental to getting a good score in the IELTS. Unless you know, and understand, what the examiners are looking for when they are marking you, it is challenging to obtain higher scores as you're not sure what is needed. To get scores of six and above, examiners look for specific things, and you can increase your score relatively quickly. In contrast, scores of five and below typically indicate the lack of, or inaccuracy of, the required elements.

我认为要想在雅思考试中拿到不错的分数，了解雅思写作评分标准非常重要。除非你知道和理解考官在阅卷的时候想要看到什么，否则很难拿到高分，因为你不知道考官需要的是什么。如果要得6分及以上分数，考官会去寻找具体的内容，你也能相对比较快速地提分。相反，如果得到5分及以下分数，通常表明评判标准中的一些要素在作文中没有体现或展示得不够准确。

*Tiny Tip:* *The overall Writing score is the average of the score of each element rounded down. For example, 6 6 5 5 is an overall score of 5.5, but so is 6 6 6 5. To get a 6, you must average 6 or more.*

**小提示：** 写作总分是每项评判标准分数的平均分的四舍五入。例如，如果四个小分分别是6、6、5、5，则总分就是5.5，但6、6、6、5也是如此。如果要拿到写作总分6分，各项平均分一定要是6分及以上。

The following section of this book will go through the criteria in detail through all four areas: Task Achievement (Task Response in Task 2), Cohesion and Coherence, Lexical Resource, Grammatical Range and Accuracy, and levels four to seven in each. Each criterion covers the Academic AND General writing tasks.

本书以下部分将详细介绍四个方面4分至7分的评分标准。四个方面为：任务完成（在Task 2中为任务回应）、衔接和连贯、词汇多样性以及语法多样性与准确性。每一个评分标准都同时涵盖学术类和培训类作文。

*Important Information:* *Unless ALL the positive criteria are met within a given score, that score CANNOT be awarded, and the examiner will look at the next level down. Many of the decisions are subjective, meaning there are no actual absolute quantities in scoring, which in turn means that each examiner's score may vary.*

**重要信息：** 除非每个分数所对应的标准都达到了，否则是拿不到这个分数的，考官就会去对应低一级分数的标准。许多决定是主观的，意味着在打分时并没有绝对的达成数量与分数的对应，所以每个考官给出的分数可能会有所不同。

*Tiny Tip:* *When looking at the criteria, also try to understand what's NOT there. This may help you understand it more.*

**小提示：** 在看写作评分标准的时候，同时需要了解什么不包含在其中，这会帮助你更好地理解它。

IELTS Examiners are trained and need to pass a test to allow them to examine candidates, and they will NOT vary in their scoring by much. However, it must be understood that examiners are human beings and will think differently occasionally.

雅思考官是经过培训的，并且需要通过一项考试，才有资格成为考官，他们在打分时不会差异太大。然而，我们必须要理解考官也是主观个体，因此他们在阅卷时偶尔会有不同的想法。

# Chapter 1 Task Achievement (Task 1) & Task Response (Task 2)
## 任务完成及任务回应

## Task Achievement (Task 1)

**Task Achievement** is about whether you effectively complete all the instructions you are given on the test paper. For Task 1, these are:

**任务完成**是指你是否有效完成题目的所有要求。在 Task 1 中，这些包含:

▶ **Write at least 150 words.** 字数不少于 150 字。

You must write enough words. If you don't, you may only receive a 5 for this part, possibly a 4 or even less. An examiner can't give anything more than this (a 6 or a 7, for example) if you don't achieve the required word count.

你必须满足最低字数要求。如果不能满足，你只能在这一项中得到 5 分，也可能是 4 分甚至更低。如果你没有达到字数要求，考官不可能给出比这个更高的分数了（如 6 分或 7 分）。

If you're unsure how many words you've written, count them by multiplying the number of words on one line by the number of lines. This can be done relatively quickly; if you think you haven't written enough, try writing some more.

如果你不确定你写了多少词，可以用一行的单词数乘以行数来计算。这是相对比较快的方法。如果你认为写得不够，可以试着再多写一些。

*Tiny Tip:* *DON'T count every single word! IT will take too much time that you could be using to write some more.*

**小提示：**不要每一个单词都数！这太浪费时间，你本可以用这段时间写更多单词。

▶ **Summarise the information by selecting and reporting the main features, and make comparisons where relevant.** 通过选择和展示主要特点来概括信息，同时对相关信息进行对比。

'Summarise' is one of the keywords here, as is 'main features'. These mean that you don't need to list every piece of data presented in the graph/map/process. For a graph or table, you will need to describe the data showing 'main trends'. For a map, it will be the main features, so not necessarily every room, side road, or flower bed. For a process, it may mean grouping some of the processes together rather than describing them individually in detail.

"概括"与"主要特点"在这一项标准中是关键词。这表明你不需要列出图表、地图或流程图中呈现的每一个数据。对于图表或表格题，你只需要描述呈现"主要趋势"的数据；对于地图题，只描述主要特征即可，所以不需要列出每一个房间、小路或是花坛；对于流程图题，只需要将几个流程分组表达清楚，而不需要详细说明每一个步骤。

'Comparisons' and 'relevant' are two more keywords that should be understood properly. When writing about a map, the task typically has two pictures: a 'now' and a 'future', or maybe a 'past' and a 'now'. As described in this book's Question Types and Approaches section, you should compare one map with the other almost entirely. This can also be said for most graphs and tables. For processes, this wouldn't be 'relevant': with a process, there is no data to compare.

"比较"和"相关"是另外两个应该正确理解的关键词。在作答地图题时，题目通常会包含两张图片，"现在"的地图和"将来"的规划图，或者"过去"和"现在"的地图。正如本书题目类型及写作方法部分中的描述，你需要把两个地图进行几乎全部的对比。这也适用于大多数图表和表格题。对于流程图题，这不一定"相关"。因为流程图题没有要进行比较的数据。

*Tiny Tip:* *DON'T compare every piece of data with every other piece of data. It will look too much like a list, and you'll write too many words without actually explaining very much.*

**小提示：**不要将每一项数据都与其他数据进行比较。这会看起来像是一个数据罗列单，而且你虽然写了很多词，但实际却没有作充分的解释。

| | Task Achievement | 任务完成 |
|---|---|---|
| Level 4 | •attempts to address the task but does not cover all key features/bullet points; the format may be inappropriate<br>•(General Training) fails to clearly explain the purpose of the letter; the tone may be inappropriate<br>•may confuse key features/bullet points with detail; parts may be unclear, irrelevant, repetitive or inaccurate | •试图就写作任务要求行文，但未能包含所有主要信息或要点；写作格式有时不恰当<br>•（培训类）未能清晰地说明信件的写作目的；行文语气有时不恰当<br>•有时混淆主要信息或要点与细节信息；部分写作内容有时不清晰、不相关、重复或不准确 |

▷ **attempts to address the task but does not cover all key features/bullet points; the format may be inappropriate** 试图就写作任务要求行文，但未能包含所有主要信息或要点；写作格式有时不恰当

This means that not all of the instructions in the task have been completed. The most commonly missed instruction is the word count. You MUST write at least 150 words; otherwise, it's likely that you'll only receive a 4 in this section. Other instructions include making comparisons, summarising information (not detailing/listing it) and reporting the 'main features', not necessarily ALL of them.

这表明题目中的要求并没有完全达成。最常见的失分点就是没有达到字数要求。你必须写至少150字。否则，在这一项评分中你很可能只能得4分。其他的要求包括比较、概括信息（不是详细列出）和展示"主要特征"，不一定要展示全部的特征。

▷ **(General Training) fails to clearly explain the purpose of the letter; the tone may be inappropriate**（培训类）未能清晰地说明信件的写作目的；行文语气有时不恰当

This refers to the lack of explaining the reason for the letter – or the 'Why?' of the letter. The 'tone' means that it may have been written as an informal letter when it should have been written formally.

这里指的是没有解释这封信的原因，即"为什么"写这封信。"语气"在这里指信件中用语的正式程度，比如本应是正式信件，但却写成了一封非正式的信件。

▷ **may confuse key features/bullet points with detail; parts may be unclear, irrelevant, repetitive or inaccurate** 有时混淆主要信息或要点与细节信息；部分写作内容有时不清晰、不相关、重复或不准确

This is best explained by using an example:
下面的例子可以最好地解释这一点：

| Task 1 Example Table | | |
|---|---|---|
| Year | Country | |
| | China | England |
| 2001 | 10 | 15 |
| 2002 | 15 | 10 |

and the student writes:

根据题目中这张表格，学生这样写：

> *In 2001, China shows 2002, and England shows 10, whereas, in 2002, China shows apples and England shows oranges.*

This sentence is a little repetitive and VERY inaccurate.

这个句子有些冗余，而且数据非常不精确。

| | Task Achievement | 任务完成 |
|---|---|---|
| Level 5 | •generally addresses the task; the format may be inappropriate in places<br>•(Academic) recounts detail mechanically with no clear overview; there may be no data to support the description<br>•(General Training) may present a purpose for the letter that is unclear at times; the tone may be variable and sometimes inappropriate<br>•presents, but inadequately covers, key features/bullet points; there may be a tendency to focus on details | •基本上能就写作任务行文；某些地方写作格式有时存在不当之处<br>•（学术类）机械地描述细节，缺乏清晰的概述；有时未能提供数据支持所描述的内容<br>•（培训类）信函有时能体现特定的写作目的，但有时目的不清晰；行文语气变化不定，且有时不得体<br>•呈现但不能充分地涵盖主要内容或要点；有时出现着重表述细节的倾向 |

❯ **generally addresses the task; the format may be inappropriate in places** 基本上能就写作任务行文；某些地方写作格式有时存在不当之处

This would mean that instructions are followed and that the formatting IS appropriate in other places.

So, as an example, most of the document is written text, but some bullet points may be added.

这表明作文基本满足题目要求，除某些地方，其余地方的写作格式是恰当的。例如，作文中大部分信息是文字形式，但在某些地方加了项目符号。

❯ **(Academic) recounts detail mechanically with no clear overview; there may be no data to support the description** （学术类）机械地描述细节，缺乏清晰的概述；有时未能提供数据支持所描述的内容

This basically means that all the candidate has done is write about the data of the table (or potentially not include the data), for example:

这里是指考生只是写出了表格的数据（甚至没有包含数据），如下例：

| Task 1 Example Table | | |
|---|---|---|
| Year | Country | |
| | China | England |
| 2001 | 10 | 15 |
| 2002 | 15 | 10 |

and the candidate writes:

考生是这样写的：

> *In 2001, China was 10, and England was 15. In 2002, China was 15, and England was 10.*
>
> *or*
>
> *In 2001, China was less, and England was more. In 2002 China was more, and England was less.*

▶ **(General Training) may present a purpose for the letter that is unclear at times; the tone may be variable and sometimes inappropriate** （培训类）信函有时能体现特定的写作目的，但有时目的不清晰；行文语气变化不定，且有时不得体

Here, the meaning is that the examiner may not clearly understand the purpose of the letter and that sometimes it's written formally, and at other times it's informal.

这项表述的意思是考官可能不清楚这封信的目的，并且信中的语气有时正式，有时不正式。

▶ **presents, but inadequately covers, key features/bullet points; there may be a tendency to focus on details** 呈现但不能充分地涵盖主要内容或要点；有时出现着重表述细节的倾向

This could mean things like missing comparisons. Remember that the task explicitly says, '***make comparisons where relevant***', so although it could be argued about which comparison was relevant, the fact that there weren't any could signify a 5.

这里表明缺少信息比较。记住，在写作任务中明确要求了"**在相关之处进行比较**"。所以，尽管对于哪些信息是相关的可能见仁见智，但如果没有体现任何比较就只能得到 5 分。

| | Task Achievement | 任务完成 |
|---|---|---|
| Level 6 | •addresses the requirements of the task<br>•(Academic) presents an overview with information appropriately selected<br>•(General Training) presents a purpose that is generally clear; there may be inconsistencies in tone<br>•presents and adequately highlights key features/bullet points but details may be irrelevant, inappropriate or inaccurate | •根据写作任务要求行文<br>•（学术类）选择恰当的信息进行概述<br>•（培训类）写作目的基本清晰；行文语气有时未能保持前后一致<br>•呈现并充分地强调了主要内容或要点，但有时含有不相关、不恰当或不准确的细节信息 |

▶ **addresses the requirements of the task 根据写作任务要求行文**

This means that all the main instructions were followed. So, the word count is above 150, comparisons have been made etc.

这里表明题目中的所有主要要求都满足。比如，字数超过150字，并且在文中进行了信息比较等。

▶ **(Academic) presents an overview with information appropriately selected（学术类）选择恰当的信息进行概述**

This is saying that the information chosen to be written about has been correctly identified. The task states, 'Summarise the information by selecting and reporting the main features ...'. Therefore, it is not required that ALL of the information is described, simply perhaps the largest and smallest, or the trend of the graph rather than each piece of data.

这里说明作文选择了恰当的信息，正如题目中所述"通过选择与描述主要特征进行概括……"。所以，不需要描述所有信息，只描述最大和最小的数据，或图表的趋势即可，而不是列出每条数据。

▶ **(General Training) presents a purpose that is generally clear; there may be inconsistencies in tone（培训类）写作目的基本清晰；行文语气有时未能保持前后一致**

'Generally clear' here means that the examiner can understand the purpose of the letter, but it still takes some effort on his/her behalf. Basically, 'generally' means 'OK' rather than 'very clear'. Again, sometimes the letter may be formal in places and informal in others, which may confuse the examiner somewhat.

"基本清晰"在这里是指考官可以理解信件的目的，但仍然需要花些工夫。通常，**generally**的意思是"还可以"，而不是"非常清晰"。同时，信件中有些地方语气正式，有些地方语气非正式，这可能会使考官产生困惑。

**presents and adequately highlights key features/bullet points but details may be irrelevant, inappropriate or inaccurate** 呈现并充分地强调了主要内容或要点，但有时含有不相关、不恰当或不准确的细节信息

This effectively means that some of the data they have written is incorrect. Remember the example from Task Achievement 4:

这里说明作文中有些数据并不准确。继续使用任务完成4分标准的例子：

| Task 1 Example Table | | |
|---|---|---|
| Year | Country | |
| | China | England |
| 2001 | 10 | 15 |
| 2002 | 15 | 10 |

and the candidate writes:

考生是这样写的：

> *Over the time period between 2001 and 2002, China grew from 12 to 15, whereas England shrank from apples to oranges.*

The difference here between a 6 and a 4 is that the formatting and key features (trend and comparison) have been successfully '**addressed**'.

6分与4分的例子区别在于，作文结构与主要特征（趋势和比较）都很好地"**体现出来了**"。

| | Task Achievement | 任务完成 |
|---|---|---|
| Level 7 | •covers the requirements of the task<br>•(Academic) presents a clear overview of main trends, differences or stages<br>•(General Training) presents a clear purpose, with the tone consistent and appropriate<br>•clearly presents and highlights key features / bullet points but could be more fully extended | •写作内容涵盖写作任务的要求<br>•（学术类）清晰地呈现关于主要趋势、区别或不同阶段的概述<br>•（培训类）清晰地呈现写作目的，行文语气一致且恰当<br>•能就主要内容或要点进行清晰的呈现与强调，但未能更为充分地展开 |

▶ **covers the requirements of the task** 写作内容涵盖写作任务的要求

This again means that all the main instructions were followed. So, the word count is above 150, comparisons have been made etc.

这里仍指作文满足了题目中所有的主要要求。比如，字数在150字以上，也对信息进行了比较。

▶ **(Academic) presents a clear overview of main trends, differences or stages**（学术类）清晰地呈现关于主要趋势、区别或不同阶段的概述

The main difference between this level and a 6 here is '*clear* overview' and '*trends, differences, or stages*'. The task must be written as an overview rather than a detailed account of the data. So, for example, in a process, rather than simply describing each step one by one, there could be a grouping of elements.

在这一项中，7分与6分的主要区别在于"**清晰地**概述"和"**主要趋势、区别或不同阶段**"。作文一定是一个总体概览，而不是对每条数据的详细描述。所以，例如在流程图题中，应该要把各个元素分组呈现，而不是简单地逐一描述每个步骤。

▶ **(General Training) presents a clear purpose, with the tone consistent and appropriate**（培训类）清晰地呈现写作目的，行文语气一致且恰当

Again the word 'clear' is mentioned here so the examiner believes that it's easy to understand the purpose and the formality is correct and remains the same throughout the letter.

这里再次提到了"清晰"这个词，表示考官认为很容易理解信件的目的，行文语气恰当，且在整封信中保持一致。

▶ **clearly presents and highlights key features/bullet points but could be more fully extended** 能就主要内容或要点进行清晰的呈现与强调，但未能更为充分地展开

'Clearly' is again emphasised, so it's essential that the examiner feels that the key features are easy to find and understand. 'Could be more fully extended' refers to the elements like comparisons that could be more detailed, for example.

"清晰"再次被强调，所以让考官觉得关键特征很容易被找到和理解是很重要的。"未能更为充分地展开"，举例来说，可以指对数据的比较更详细一些。

## ⊙ Task Response (Task 2)

*Task Response* is about whether you effectively complete all the instructions you are given on the test paper. For Task 2, these are:

**任务回应**是指你是否有效地完成了试卷上给你的所有要求。对于 Task 2，这些包括：

▶ **Write at least 250 words. 字数最少为 250 字。**

You must write enough words. If you don't, you may only receive a 5 for this part, possibly a 4 or even less. An examiner can't give anything more than this (a 6 or a 7, for example) if you don't achieve the required word count.

你必须写够字数。如果不能满足字数要求，这一项你只能得 5 分，可能 4 分甚至更低。如果你没有达到要求的字数，考官不能给更高的分数（如 6 分或 7 分）。

If you're unsure how many words you've written, count them by multiplying the number of words on one line by the number of lines. This can be done relatively quickly; if you think you haven't written enough, try writing some more.

如果你不确定写了多少单词，可以用一行的单词数乘以行数来计算，这可以相对比较快地完成。如果你认为写得不够，那就尝试再多写一些。

> *Tiny Tip:* *DON'T count every single word! IT will take too much time that you could be using to write some more.*
>
> **小提示：**不要每一个单词都数！这样会浪费太多时间，而你可以用这个时间写更多单词。

The essay question. This can be one of the following:

作文题目，举例如下：

a. Discuss both these views and give your own opinion.

b. To what extent do you agree or disagree?

c. Is this a positive or negative development?

The above are the most common questions but could also cover cause and effect essays. So you may get questions like:

以上是最常见的题目，但你也可能遇见下面这些包含因果关系的作文题目：

a. What do you think are the causes of this problem?

b. What measures could be taken to solve it?

> *Tiny Tip:* *Although the words or phrases may differ, quite often, they're asking for the same thing. Once you figure out what the question is asking, you'll be able to understand what kind of essay you'll write.*

▶ Give reasons for your answer and include any relevant examples from your own knowledge or experience. 请为你的答案给出理由，并将你自己的知识或经验中任何相关的例子包括在内。

This is asking you to provide supporting evidence in your paragraphs. If you don't include this element, it's doubtful that you'll be awarded the higher scores.

这类题目是要求你在段落中提供支持性证据。如果你的作文中没有包含这个元素，那你很难得到更高的分数。

| | Task Response | 任务回应 |
|---|---|---|
| Level 4 | •responds to the task only in a minimal way or the answer is tangential; the format maybe inappropriate<br>•presents a position but this is unclear<br>•presents some main ideas but these are difficult to identify and may be repetitive, irrelevant or not well supported | • 仅最低限度地回应了写作任务，或所答相关性不大；写作格式有时不甚恰当<br>• 提出了一个观点但并不清晰<br>• 提出了一些主要论点但难以在文中确认，且这些观点可能重复、不相关或缺乏论据支持 |

▶ **responds to the task only in a minimal way 仅最低限度地回应了写作任务**

To me, this would mean that only one of the required elements has been completed.

对我来说，这意味着只完成了一项所要求的任务。

▶ **... or the answer is tangential 或所答相关性不大**

This is a little more difficult to understand. By 'tangential', it means that your answer isn't about the same topic as the original question.

这有点难理解。"相关性不大"的意思是文不对题，你的答案与题目要求讨论的话题并不相符。

For example, if the question asks you about 'communication technologies' and you write an essay about apps on your smartphone – they don't match. Although smartphones are indeed a form of communication technology, it's only one. There are many others, including telephones, email, satellites, etc., and if your essay focuses purely on Smartphone apps, it is not really what was intended by the question.

例如，如果题目中请你谈谈"通信技术"，而你写的是一篇关于智能手机上的应用程序的文章，它们就不匹配。虽然智能手机确实是一种通信技术，但它只是一种。通信技术还包含很多，比如电话、电子邮件、卫星等。如果你的作文只关注智能手机应用程序，这并不是这个题目的真正意图。

▶ **... the format maybe inappropriate 写作格式有时不甚恰当**

The style, or format, of the text maybe be wrong for what you're trying to do. For example, you wouldn't want to include a table or bullet points, open the text in a letter format, etc.

你的作文风格或格式可能不恰当。例如，在一封书信中，不应该包含表格或项目符号等。

▶ **presents a position but this is unclear 提出了一个观点但并不清晰**

This means that the examiner realises what side of the argument you are taking or what you are trying to say, but it's not clear, and he needs to work at understanding your message.

这意味着考官能看出来你支持哪一方观点或者你想说什么，但表达不清晰，他需要费点力去理解你的信息。

▶ **presents some main ideas but these are difficult to identify and may be repetitive, irrelevant** 提出了一些主要论点但难以在文中确认，且这些观点可能重复、不相关

This is where the examiner finds it challenging to either find, or identify your ideas within the text, you repeat them or that they aren't relevant to the question/statement that has been given.

考官认为在上下文中很难找到，或者识别出你的观点，你只是在重复它们，或者它们与题目信息不相关。

▶ **... or not well supported** 或缺乏论据支持

This means that you haven't given any examples or data to support your initial statement.

这意味着你没有给出任何例子或数据来支持你最初的陈述。

| | Task Response | 任务回应 |
|---|---|---|
| Level 5 | •addresses the task only partially; the format may be inappropriate in places <br>•expresses a position but the development is not always clear and there may be no conclusions drawn <br>•presents some main ideas but these are limited and not sufficiently developed; there may be irrelevant detail | •仅回应了部分写作任务；写作格式有时在某些地方不甚恰当 <br>•表述了一个观点，但展开论证过程未能保持一贯清晰，且可能缺乏结论 <br>•提出一些主要论点但十分有限，且未能充分展开论证；有时出现无关细节 |

▶ **addresses the task only partially** 仅回应了部分写作任务

There is an improvement on Level 4, but maybe only two of the three instructions have been completed here.

相较于4分，这里有所提升，但可能只完成了题目所要求的三个指示中的两个。

▶ **... the format may be inappropriate in places** 写作格式有时在某些地方不甚恰当

Again, an improvement. Rather than the format being completely wrong, it's only incorrect sometimes. This may mean that only certain sentences or maybe one of the paragraphs may be incorrect.

同样，相较于4分是有提升，格式并不是完全错误，只是有时不正确。这意味着只有某些句子或段落可能出现了错误。

▶ **expresses a position but the development is not always clear and there may be no conclusions drawn** 表述了一个观点，但展开论证过程未能保持一贯清晰，且可能缺乏结论

This criterion is fairly self-explanatory. Here the examiner can identify your position, but not always easily, and you may not have written a conclusion.

这个标准是不言自明的。考官可以确定你的立场，但并不总是很容易，而且你可能没有写结论。

▶ **presents some main ideas but these are limited and not sufficiently developed; there may be irrelevant detail** 提出一些主要论点但十分有限，且未能充分展开论证；有时出现无关细节

The main key phrase here is 'not sufficiently developed'. This means that when you have put forward an argument, you do not explain it clearly or add supporting evidence, like an example.

这里的关键词语是"未能充分展开"，意思是你虽然提出了一个论点，但没有清晰地解释，或添加支持例证。

| | Task Response | 任务回应 |
|---|---|---|
| Level 6 | •addresses all parts of the task although some parts may be more fully covered than others<br>•presents a relevant position although the conclusions may become unclear or repetitive<br>•presents relevant main ideas but some may be inadequately developed/unclear | •回应了各部分写作任务，但某些部分的论证可能比其他部分更为充分<br>•提出了一个切题的观点，尽管各种结论有时不甚清晰或重复<br>•提出了多个相关的主要论点，但某些论点可能未能充分展开进行论证或不甚清晰 |

▶ **addresses all parts of the task although some parts may be more fully covered than others** 回应了各部分写作任务，但某些部分的论证可能比其他部分更为充分

This is saying that you have covered all the instructions, but maybe some examples are a little short, or there's only one example in the essay rather than two.

这里说明你的作文涵盖了题目中的所有指示，但有些例子有点短，或者在作文中只有一个例子而不是两个。

▶ **presents a relevant position although the conclusions may become unclear or repetitive** 提出了一个切题的观点，尽管各种结论有时不甚清晰或重复

This means that although the examiner understands your point of view in the text, they may not understand the conclusion. It may contrast your previous positions.

这意味着考官虽然明白你在作文中的观点，但可能不能理解你的结论。有可能结论与之前的观点是不一致的。

▶ **presents relevant main ideas but some may be inadequately developed/unclear** 提出了多个相关的主要论点，但某些论点可能未能充分展开进行论证或不甚清晰

This part is saying that there aren't enough supporting evidence/examples in your paragraphs, or the examiner is having trouble understanding them.

这里的意思是你在作文的段落中没有足够的证据或例子支持论点，或者考官认为证据或例子不太容易理解。

| | Task Response | 任务回应 |
|---|---|---|
| Level 7 | •addresses all parts of the task<br>•presents a clear position throughout the response<br>•presents, extends and supports main ideas, but there may be a tendency to overgeneralise and/or supporting ideas may lack focus | •回应各部分写作任务<br>•回应写作任务过程中始终呈现一个清晰的观点<br>•呈现、发展主要论点并就其进行论证，但有时出现过于一概而论的倾向和（或）论据缺乏重点的倾向 |

▶ **addresses all parts of the task 回应各部分写作任务**

This is self-explanatory and means that all instructions are covered correctly.

不言自明，这里指作文涵盖了题目中的所有指示。

▶ **presents a clear position throughout the response 回应写作任务过程中始终呈现一个清晰的观点**

This, again, is fairly simple to understand, but the keyword 'throughout' is very important. It means that your position is given and understood all the way through the text. To me, this means that it includes the introduction, body and conclusion.

这条也比较容易理解，但这里的关键词 throughout 很重要。这意味着在整篇作文中，你能给出观点，并且贯穿始终，并能清晰理解。对我来说，这代表它包括开头、主体段和结论。

▶ **presents, extends and supports main ideas, but there may be a tendency to overgeneralise and/or supporting ideas may lack focus 呈现、发展主要论点并就其进行论证，但有时出现过于一概而论的倾向和（或）论据缺乏重点的倾向**

This is saying that although there is evidence and/or examples in the given text, they are not specific enough. For example:

这是说虽然在作文中有证据和/或例子，但它们不够具体。例如：

> *A plane landed.*

The above is too general and creates more questions than it answers. What plane? When and where did it land? Etc.

上面这个例子太宽泛了，读的时候会使人产生更多问题。比如，什么飞机？它在何时何地降落等等。

> *The Boeing 777 landed in Beijing Wednesday evening on time.*

In this second example, all the questions from the first statement are answered. This example would be considered specific.

在第二个例子中，刚刚提出的所有问题都得到了回答。这个例子就可以被视为是具体的。

# Chapter 2 Cohesion and Coherence
## 衔接和连贯

The Cohesion and Coherence section for Task 1 is the same as Task 2.

Task 1 中衔接和连贯的标准与 Task 2 的相同。

***Cohesion and Coherence*** are the 'glue' of the text and the 'logic' that brings the essay together.

**衔接和连贯**是文本内容的"粘合剂",也是贯穿文章的"逻辑"。

### ▶ Cohesion 衔接

If something is 'cohesive', it is 'united and works together effectively', as defined by the online Cambridge Dictionary. This means the passage flows easily from between paragraphs as well as between and within sentences.

根据剑桥在线词典的定义,如果某物是"cohesive",即有凝聚力,它是"团结一致,有效地协同工作"。这意味着文章在段落之间、句子之间和句子内部都很流畅连贯。

Cohesive devices are words like 'and', 'but', or 'because'. They are also phrases like 'in addition', 'at first' or 'in conclusion'. It's essential that these kinds of 'signposting' words and phrases are used so that it is easy for the examiner to understand which data is together and which is separate.

衔接手段是像 and、but 或 because 这样的词,也指如 in addition、at first 或 in conclusion 这样的短语。使用这些"路标"式的词汇和短语是很重要的,这样考官就会很容易理解哪些数据是放到一起的,哪些没有。

| Task 1 Example Table | | |
|---|---|---|
| **Year** | **Country** | |
| | **China** | **England** |
| 2001 | 10 | 15 |
| 2002 | 15 | 10 |

**· Example 1 – Bad ·**

*2001 China 10. 2001 England 15. 2002 China 15. 2002 England 10.*

· Example 2 – Better ·

*In 2001, China shows 10, and England shows 15, whereas in 2002, China shows 15 and then England shows 10.*

You can see from the first example that, firstly, they aren't correct or complete sentences, and secondly, it is very much a stop-and-start rhythm. In the second example, however, the use of 'and' and 'whereas' connects the data together and makes the whole sentence flow a little better.

从 Example 1 中可以看到，第一这些句子是错的、不完整的，第二，每个句子被切分得非常短，是一个即止又启的节奏。但在 Example 2 中，and 和 whereas 的使用将数据连接到一起，使整个句子读起来更加流畅。

· Example 3 – Bad ·

*I agree with w. I don't think that y is good. I think x is great. On second thoughts, I don't like w after all.*

· Example 4 – Better ·

*I agree with w, but I don't think that y is good, and I think x is great. On second thoughts, I don't like w after all.*

In the fourth example, however, the use of 'and' and 'but' connects the information together and makes the whole sentence flow a little better. We'll deal with the logical order in the next section.

在 Example 4 中，and 和 but 的使用将句了的信息连在了一起，使整个句子更加流畅。我们在下一部分会详细说明关于逻辑顺序的要求。

## ▶ Coherence 连贯

'If an argument, set of ideas, or a plan is coherent, it is clear and carefully considered, and each part of it connects or follows in a natural or reasonable way' is the Online Cambridge Dictionary definition. Simply put, this is the 'logic' of the passage.

剑桥在线词典对 coherence 的定义是，"如果一个论点、一套想法或一个计划是连贯的，它是清晰且经过仔细考虑的，它的每一部分都以一种自然或合理的方式联系或遵循。"简单说，就是指文章的"逻辑"。

If your text is arranged in what the examiner feels is a logical way, you will score higher marks than if your description of the data jumps around and is difficult to trace, or follow.

相较于数据在文章中跳来跳去地出现，让读者难以跟上，如果考官认为你的文章内容组织很有逻辑，你的得分会更高。

Using the table below as our data:

用下面这张表格题目举例：

| Task 1 Example Table | | |
|---|---|---|
| Year | Country | |
| | China | England |
| 2001 | 10 | 15 |
| 2002 | 15 | 10 |

**· Example 1 – Bad ·**

*In 2002, England shows 10. In 2001, China shows 10.*

**· Example 2 – Better ·**

*In 2001, China shows 10, and England shows 15.*

In the first example, the first data that is mentioned is in the bottom right corner of the table. This doesn't seem like a very logical place to start. However, the 'better' example begins at what many people would consider the first piece of data.

Example 1 中提到的第一个数据位于表格右下角，从这里开始似乎不太合乎逻辑。而"更好"的例子是从人们都认为应当是第一个的数据开始。

**· Example 3 – Bad ·**

*I agree with w... I don't think that y is good... I think x is great. On second thoughts, I don't like w after all.*

**· Example 4 – Better ·**

*I agree with w, and I think x is great.*
*On the other hand, I don't think that y and z are any good.*

You can see from the fourth example that there's logical grouping in the sentences (potentially paragraphs) – agree/good and disagree/bad rather than the mixing and order problems in the third example.

在 Example 4 中，句子之间（也可能是段落之间）有逻辑分组——同意或好和不同意或坏，而不像在 Example 3 中，逻辑和顺序都混乱。

Another element that is measured within this section is 'referencing' in the 5 and 6 scores. It simply refers to the use of pronouns like 'it', 'this', 'they' etc. Using the data above as an example:

在连贯这一部分中另一个测评要素是5分和6分的评分标准中的"referencing"，即指代。简单说就是如 it、this、they 等代词的使用。以上面表格中的数据举例：

**· Example 1 – No referencing 没有代词指代 ·**

*There are two countries shown. The countries are China and England.*

**· Example 2 – With referencing 有代词指代 ·**

*There are two countries shown. **They** are China and England.*

*Important Tip:* *The main difference between Task 2 and Task 1 in this criterion is the addition of examining the use of paragraphing in the text. This starts at level 4 and is mentioned all the way up to level 9.*

**重要提示：** 在这一标准中，Task 2 和 Task 1 的一个主要区别就是增加了对段落在文章中的使用的检查。从 4 分到 9 分的标准都包括这一项。

| | Cohesion and Coherence | 衔接和连贯 |
|---|---|---|
| Level 4 | •presents information and ideas but these are not arranged coherently and there is no clear progression in the response<br>•uses some basic cohesive devices but these may be inaccurate or repetitive<br>•may not write in paragraphs or their use may be confusing **(only for Task 2)** | •呈现了信息及观点，但未能连贯地组织这些信息及观点，且未能清晰地推进行文发展<br>•使用了一些基本的衔接手段，但有时出现不准确或重复的使用<br>•没有使用段落写作，或段落使用造成疑惑（只适用于 Task 2） |

▶ **presents information and ideas but these are not arranged coherently and there is no clear progression in the response** 呈现了信息及观点，但未能连贯地组织这些信息及观点，且未能清晰地推进行文发展

For Task 1, this means that the data in the passage is not arranged in a logical way, and it doesn't clearly flow from one part of the data to the next. An excellent example of this would be the bad example I used on the page 22.

针对 Task 1，这意味着文章中的数据没有以逻辑方式排列，并且数据之间的衔接也不清晰流畅。一个贴切的例子就是我在第 22 页中举过的例子。

For Task 2, this means that the ideas in the passage are not arranged logically, and it doesn't clearly flow from one part of the essay to the next. An excellent example of this might be where advantages and disadvantages are mentioned in the same paragraph.

针对 Task 2，这里指文章中的观点安排没有逻辑性，而且上下文衔接也不清晰流畅。一个很好的例子是在同一个段落里既有优点的论证，也有缺点的论证。

▶ **uses some basic cohesive devices but these may be inaccurate or repetitive** 使用了一些基本的衔接手段，但有时出现不准确或重复的使用

'Basic' cohesive devices could be considered as words like 'and', 'or', and 'but'. If these are used too much, or they're used incorrectly, a 4 will be given.

"基本"衔接手段可以指如 and、or 和 but 这样的词。如果这些词用的频率太高，或者使用不得当，那就会得 4 分。

· Example ·

| Year | Country | |
|---|---|---|
| | China | England |
| 2001 | 10 | 15 |
| 2002 | 15 | 10 |

> *In 2001 China showed 10 and England, and in 2002 China showed 15, and England showed 10.*
> *And...*

In this example, 'and' is overused.

在这个例子中，and 一词的使用次数就过多。

▶ **may not write in paragraphs or their use may be confusing (only for Task 2)** 没有使用段落写作，或段落使用造成疑惑（只适用于 Task 2）

This is the beginning of the additions mentioned a little earlier in the book and where Task 2 criteria differ from Task 1. This part is reasonably easy to understand. It means that either the examiner is confused by the paragraph usage – maybe a candidate starts a new paragraph in the middle of a sentence – or they simply don't use paragraphing to break up the essay.

这是本书前面提到的补充内容，也是 Task 2 的标准与 Task 1 不同的地方。这部分比较容易理解。它的意思是段落的排列方式使考官困惑，既可能是考生在一个句子的中间开始了一个新的段落，又或者他们没有给作文分段。

*Tiny Tip:* *Make sure you CLEARLY leave a space between your paragraphs. You'll likely get a 4 for this part if you don't. Indenting the first line of each paragraph would also be a good idea.*

**小提示：**一定要记得在段落之间留一行空行。如果段落之间没有留行，你可能只能得 4 分。缩进每段的第一行也是个好主意。

| | Cohesion and Coherence | 衔接和连贯 |
|---|---|---|
| Level 5 | •presents information with some organisation but there may be a lack of overall progression<br>•makes inadequate, inaccurate or over-use of cohesive devices<br>•may be repetitive because of lack of referencing and substitution<br>•may not write in paragraphs, or paragraphing may be inadequate **(only for Task 2)** | •有一定组织性地呈现信息，但有时缺乏清晰的总体行文推进<br>•衔接手段不足、不准确或过度使用<br>•由于指代和替换不足显得行文重复<br>•没有使用段落写作，或者分段不足（只适用于 Task 2） |

**▶ presents information with some organisation but there may be a lack of overall progression** 有一定组织性地呈现信息，但有时缺乏清晰的总体行文推进

Here the examiner believes that although there is 'some organisation', it doesn't flow easily, and things may be out of order.

在这里，考官认为虽然文章内容有"一定的组织性"，但信息衔接不流畅，内容可能是无序的。

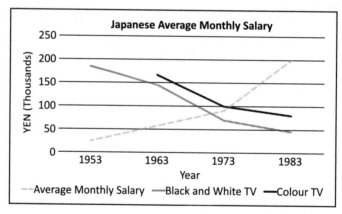

If you were to describe Black and White TVs, then Average Monthly Salary, then Colour TVs, it wouldn't really be particularly logical. The TVs should be grouped together, and the Monthly salary should remain separate. This element is somewhat based on what YOU believe is logical, so opinions may vary slightly, but it would generally not affect scoring much.

例如，在描述这张表格时，如果你先描述黑白电视，然后是平均月薪，然后再描述彩色电视，那就不太合乎逻辑。因为电视的数据应该放到一起分析，平均月薪的数据单独分析。这项标准在一定程度上是基于你认为什么是符合逻辑的，所以每个人的意见可能会稍有不同，但通常不会对得分产生太大影响。

> **makes inadequate, inaccurate or over-use of cohesive devices** 衔接手段不足、不准确或过度使用

Cohesive devices are words like 'and', 'but', or 'because'. They are also phrases like 'in addition', 'on the one hand' or 'as a result of this'. If there aren't any, or what is used is incorrect or simply they use the same one all the time, it would be considered a 5. Look at the example sentence below:

衔接手段是像 and、but 或 because 这样的词汇，还有如 in addition、on the one hand 或 as a result of this 这样的短语。如果在文章中没有使用，或者使用不得当，或者全篇一直使用相同的表达，就会得5分。如下例：

> *In 2001, vegetables went up and in 2002 they went down and in 2003 they fell and in 2004 they fell more. However, they went down in 2005.*

You can see here that there are too many 'and' and the 'However' is used incorrectly. It would rate more than 4, because 'however' could be considered not "**basic**".

你可以看到，在这个例子中 and 使用的次数太多，而 however 一词的用法也不正确。但得分比4分高，是因为 however 可以不算是 "**基本**" 词汇。

> **may be repetitive because of lack of referencing and substitution** 由于指代和替换不足显得行文重复

The most basic form of referencing and substitution is to use pronouns (he/she/it/they/that etc). Look at the example sentence below referring to the previous graph:

最基本的指代和替换方式是使用代词（he、she、it、they、that 等）。下面是描述上一个图表的例句：

> *Black and White TV's were about 180k Yen in 1953, and in 1963 Black and White TV's had fallen to around 150k Yen. By 1973, Black and White TV's were approximately 75k Yen.*

Black and White TV's is simply repeated. There is no 'they'. An example including referencing would look like this:

Black and White TV 只是简单地重复，没有用 they 来替换。包含指代替换的例子如下：

> *Black and White TV's were about 180k Yen in 1953, and in 1963 they had fallen to around 150k Yen. By 1973, they were approximately 75k Yen.*

Look at the example sentence below:

见下例：

> *People that believe this do x, and people that believe this also do y.*

In this example, the second 'people that believe this' could be replaced by 'they'.

在这个例子中，第二个 people that believe this 可以用 they 代替。

▶ **may not write in paragraphs, or paragraphing may be inadequate (only for Task 2)** 没有使用段落写作，或者分段不足（只适用于 Task 2）

The main difference between this and Level 4 is 'inadequate' versus 'confusing'. Both indicate that paragraphing attempts are being made, but, for me at least, with 'confusing', I would ask, "Why have you written a new paragraph there?" whereas with 'inadequate', I would ask, "Why are there only two paragraphs?"

相较于 4 分标准中提到的分段"使人困惑"，这里是分段"不足"。两者都表明考生在作文中尝试分段，但至少对我来说，当考官感到"困惑"的时候，我会问："为什么你在那里写了一个新的段落？"但对于"不足"，我会问："为什么只有两段？"

| | Cohesion and Coherence | 衔接和连贯 |
|---|---|---|
| Level 6 | •arranges information and ideas coherently and there is a clear overall progression<br>•uses cohesive devices effectively, but cohesion within and/or between sentences may be faulty or mechanical<br>•may not always use referencing clearly or appropriately<br>•uses paragraphing, but not always logically **(only for Task 2)** | •连贯地组织信息及观点，能清晰地推进总体行文发展<br>•有效地使用衔接手段，但句内和（或）句间的衔接有时有误或过于机械<br>•有时无法保持一贯清晰或恰当地使用指代<br>•使用段落写作，但未能保持段落间的逻辑（**只适用于 Task 2**） |

▶ **arranges information and ideas coherently and there is a clear overall progression** 连贯地组织信息及观点，能清晰地推进总体行文发展

What is meant here is that the text is arranged logically and that there is an apparent flow between one idea and the next. This is 'clearly' recognisable. Whereas in Level 5, there was '**some organisation**', it is much improved in Level 6.

这里是指文章内容的安排有逻辑性，每一个观点之间的衔接也清晰流畅，是可以很"清晰地"识别的。而在5分标准中，只是"**有一定组织性地呈现信息**"，因此在这一项中6分相较于5分有很大提升。

▶ **uses cohesive devices effectively, but cohesion within and/or between sentences may be faulty or mechanical** 有效地使用衔接手段，但句内和（或）句间的衔接有时有误或过于机械

This describes the fact that '**cohesive devices**' are used (and, but, however, etc.) but not always correctly, and that between some sentences or paragraphs, the 'glue' might be a bit weak, or repetitive.

这里是指使用了"**衔接手段**"（如 and、but、however 等），但用法不总是正确。并且，在句子或段落之间，文章的"粘合性"有些弱，或者衔接手段使用比较重复。

▶ **may not always use referencing clearly or appropriately** 有时无法保持一贯清晰或恰当地使用指代

This element is relatively self-explanatory. The main difference between Level 5 and Level 6 here, is that in Level 5, the candidate wasn't using referencing. In Level 6, they are at least trying to use it, sometimes successfully, sometimes not.

这个要素相对来说是不言自明的。在这一要素中，5分和6分评分标准的最大区别是，在5分中，

考生并没有使用指代。但在6分中，他们至少尝试使用指代，虽然有时用得正确，有时不正确。

▶ **uses paragraphing, but not always logically (only for Task 2)** 使用段落写作，但未能保持段落间的逻辑（只适用于 Task 2）

This, I believe, is self-explanatory. It shows that the candidate attempts to use paragraphing but not always correctly/logically.

我认为，这条也很清楚。这表明虽然考生尝试用段落写作，但并不总是正确或符合逻辑。

| | Cohesion and Coherence | 衔接和连贯 |
|---|---|---|
| Level 7 | •logically organises information and ideas; there is clear progression throughout<br>•uses a range of cohesive devices appropriately although there may be some under-/over-use<br>•presents a clear central topic within each paragraph **(only for Task 2)** | •符合逻辑地组织信息及观点；清晰的行文推进贯穿全文<br>•恰当地使用一系列衔接手段，尽管有时使用不足或过多<br>•每个段落均有一个清晰的中心主题（**只适用于 Task 2**） |

▶ **logically organises information and ideas; there is clear progression throughout** 符合逻辑地组织信息及观点；清晰的行文推进贯穿全文

The main difference here between a 6 and a 7 is '***clear*** progression ***throughout***'. So, there are two items here that need to be understood. The first is '***clear***'. This means that it's easy to follow and is obviously in a correct order/grouping. The second part, '***throughout***', means that in 'all' of the essay, not just in parts.

这里6分和7分的主要区别是"**清晰**行文推进**贯穿**全文"。在这里，有两个概念需要理解。第一个是"**清晰的**"。这意味着文章很容易读下去，而且很明显是有正确的顺序或分组。第二个是"**贯穿**"，即指是应用在"整篇"文章中，而不只是文章的部分位置。

▶ **uses a range of cohesive devices appropriately although there may be some under-/over-use** 恰当地使用一系列衔接手段，尽管有时使用不足或过多

Here we are looking at an improvement on 6. Whereas 5 is saying 'doesn't use them', 6 is saying 'uses them, but sometimes incorrectly', here at 7 it's saying 'good range, and mostly correct although some may be repetitive or not used at all'.

这里我们看到的是相较于6分的提升。在5分中提到"没有使用衔接手段"，6分提到"使用衔接手段，但有时使用不正确"，在7分中，则是"恰当地使用一系列衔接手段，尽管有时重复或使用不足"。

▶ **presents a clear central topic within each paragraph (only for Task 2)** 每个段落均有一个清晰的中心主题（只适用于 Task 2）

This means that paragraphing not only exists but is clearly defined and has only one clear topic within it. Examiners will check whether there is a clear topic sentence and also whether the evidence/example correctly supports that statement.

这里指作文不仅有分段，而且段落划分明确，同时只有一个明确的主题贯穿其中。考官会查看是否有一个明确的主旨句，以及证据或例子是否恰当地支持该陈述。

# Chapter 3  Lexical Resource
## 词汇多样性

The Lexical Resource section for Task 1 is the same as Task 2.

Task 1的词汇多样性标准与Task 2相同。

*Lexical Resource* is a more formal way of saying Vocabulary. This section of the criteria is all about the words you use and whether you can use paraphrasing/synonyms to explain your ideas precisely and in detail.

词汇多样性是Vocabulary（词汇）的一个更正式的说法。这部分的标准是关于你所使用的单词，以及你是否可以用转述或同义词准确而详细地解释你的想法。

In IELTS Writing, Lexical Resource means changing a word from a noun to a verb, like 'deployment' to 'deploy', or even tenses, like moving from the Past to the Future tense. It is also the range of vocabulary that you have and can use when writing about both 'Familiar' and 'Unfamiliar' topics.

在雅思写作考试中，词汇多样性指的是把名词变成动词，如deployment转为deploy，或改变时态，如从过去时变成将来时。这也是你在写"熟悉"和"不熟悉"的话题时可以使用的词汇范围。

As we go through the different criteria levels, you'll notice that 'word formation' and 'range' are used a lot. In my view, it's of paramount importance that when you are studying vocabulary, you also learn as many different synonyms as you can and how to use them. The online Cambridge Dictionary defines a paraphrase as 'to repeat something written or spoken using different words, often in a humorous form or in a simpler and shorter form that makes the original meaning clearer'.

当我们在逐级看这些标准时，你会注意到"构词"和"词汇范围"出现了很多次。我认为最重要的是，当你学习词汇时，也要尽可能多地学习不同的同义词以及如何使用它们。剑桥在线词典对"转述"的定义是："对写下来或说出来的内容用不同的词再次表达，通常以幽默的形式，或者以更简单、更简短的形式，使原意更清晰。"

Important Information: *Although synonyms and paraphrases are technically different, they are often measured similarly by examiners. So, what this means is that if you can use other words to explain something, it would be included as a paraphrase. If you use different words than in the question asked, it would be a good thing.*

**重要信息：**虽然同义词和转述在理念上不一样，但考官常会以相似的标准来衡量。所以，这意味着如果你可以用其他词来解释某事，这就可以被理解为是转述。如果你用的词和题目中的不一样，那是件好事。

|  | **Lexical Resource** | 词汇多样性 |
|---|---|---|
| Level 4 | •uses only basic vocabulary which may be used repetitively or which may be inappropriate for the task<br>•has limited control of word formation and/or spelling<br>•errors may cause strain for the reader | •只使用基本词汇，且有时重复使用这些词汇或使用对于写作任务来说不恰当的词汇<br>•对构词和（或）拼写掌握有限<br>•错误可能对读者造成阅读困难 |

▶ **uses only basic vocabulary which may be used repetitively or which may be inappropriate for the task** 只使用基本词汇，且有时重复使用这些词汇或使用对于写作任务来说不恰当的词汇

This means that the words used are too repetitive.

这意味着使用的词语过于重复。

**· Example 1 ·**

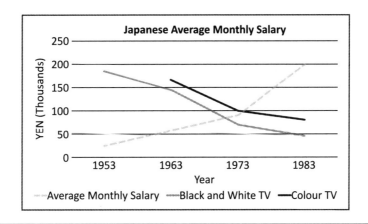

*In 1953 it was 25. In 1963 it **went up**. In 1973 it **went up**, and in 1983 it also **went up**.*

'went up' is used repetitively and would be considered 'basic' vocabulary.

went up这个短语被反复使用，而且只能算是 "基本" 词汇。

For Task 2, this means that the words used are too repetitive or they are the wrong words that can distort the intended meaning.

针对 Task 2，这里指词汇的使用过于重复，或者使用了不恰当的词汇，导致意思不清楚。

**· Example 2 ·**

*Some people advantage that ...*

In this example, 'advantage' is being used incorrectly, 'believe' or 'think' would be more appropriate.

在上例中，advantage 的使用不正确，如果用 believe 或 think 会更合适。

▶ **has limited control of word formation and/or spelling** 对构词和（或）拼写掌握有限

'Word formation' refers to changing between different tenses, or maybe a noun to an adjective.

"构词"是指在不同的时态之间转化，或者是由名词到形容词的变化。

· Example ·

*go → gone or go → went and creation → creative*

'Spelling' means whether or not you have correctly spelt the words you have written/typed.

"拼写"是指你是否能正确写出或打出单词。

▶ **errors may cause strain for the reader** 错误可能对读者造成阅读困难

Here, it's up to the examiner what 'strain' means, and it may differ between examiners. As a rule of thumb, I feel that if the word needs to be read more than twice, it deserves a 4.

在这里，"阅读困难"指什么取决于考官，而每个考官的解释可能会有所不同。根据经验，我认为如果一个单词需要读两遍以上，就只能得4分。

| | Lexical Resource | 词汇多样性 |
|---|---|---|
| Level 5 | • uses a limited range of vocabulary, but this is minimally adequate for the task<br>• may make noticeable errors in spelling and/or word formation that may cause some difficulty for the reader | • 使用词汇范围有限，但能达到进行写作任务的最低限度<br>• 在拼写和（或）构词方面可能出现明显的错误，且可能会对读者造成一定的阅读困难 |

▶ **uses a limited range of vocabulary, but this is minimally adequate for the task** 使用词汇范围有限，但能达到进行写作任务的最低限度

This partially is a judgement call as there is no definitive number for 'limited range'. Normally, if the candidate isn't using synonyms and simply repeating verbs/nouns used in the question and little else, a 5 would be necessary.

这在一定程度上需要判断，因为"词汇范围有限"没有明确的数字。通常情况下，如果考生没有使用同义词，只是简单地重复题目中的动词或名词，只会得到 5 分。

▶ **may make noticeable errors in spelling and/or word formation that may cause some difficulty for the reader** 在拼写和（或）构词方面可能出现明显的错误，且可能会对读者造成一定的阅读困难

In this element, it means that there are glaring errors in spelling, and they make you think twice. As a general 'rule of thumb', if it needs to be read twice, it is causing you '***some difficulty***'.

在这一项中，指的是在拼写中出现明显错误，需要读者读两遍才理解。通常的原则是，如果一篇文章需要读两遍，就会造成"**一定的阅读困难**"，只会得 5 分。

**· Example ·**

> *This sentens is spilled wrong on purpos. Although some wurds are spilt wurs then othurs.*

The above, I would class as a 5, although if you have to read it more than twice to understand it, you may consider a 4.

上面这个例句，我会打 5 分。但如果你需要读两遍以上才能理解这句话，你可以考虑给 4 分。

Word formation is basically changing the Noun into an Adjective or a Verb into a Noun. It refers to tenses as well. Again, if you have to read it twice before you understand it, it would class as a 5.

构词基本上说就是把名词变成形容词，或把动词变成名词，它也指时态的转换。同样，如果你需要读两遍才能理解，那一般只会得 5 分。

| | Lexical Resource | 词汇多样性 |
|---|---|---|
| Level 6 | •uses an adequate range of vocabulary for the task<br>•attempts to use less common vocabulary but with some inaccuracy<br>•makes some errors in spelling and/or word formation, but they do not impede communication | •使用足够的词汇开展写作任务<br>•试图使用不常用词汇，但有时使用不准确<br>•在拼写和（或）构词方面有错误，但不影响交流 |

▶ **uses an adequate range of vocabulary for the task** 使用足够的词汇开展写作任务

The meaning here is that the candidate is using synonyms/paraphrases in the text, and more than simply one. Again, there is no fixed number that would indicate 'range', is up to the examiner to judge it.

这里的意思是考生在文章中使用同义词或转述，而且不只一处。同样，没有固定的数字来表示"范围"，这取决于考官的判断。

▶ **attempts to use less common vocabulary but with some inaccuracy** 试图使用不常用词汇，但有时使用不准确

'Less common vocabulary' means words that EFL Learners, or even natives, wouldn't necessarily use every day. For example, some common words would include:

"不常用词汇"指的是英语学习者，甚至是母语人士，不一定每天都使用的词汇。例如，一些常见的单词包括：

> *speak, say, talk*

Whereas 'less common' versions of these words would be:

而这些单词的"不常用"版本是：

> *discuss, chat, converse*

Even if the candidate gets 'some' of the efforts wrong, they're still trying, which would bring them into the 6 rather than the 5.

即使考生做了"一些"不恰当的尝试，但仍能看出他们在尝试，这会得6分，而不是5分。

▶ **makes some errors in spelling and/or word formation, but they do not impede communication** 在拼写和（或）构词方面有错误，但不影响交流

So here, the difference is whether you would need to read the words twice in order to understand them. Using the example we had in Level 5, but at Level 6:

所以，这里的区别在于你是否需要读两遍才能理解它们。使用我们在解释5分的标准时用到的例子，按照6分的标准，句子可以如下：

> *This sentence is spelled wrong on purpose. Although some wurds are spelled wurse than others.*

Although, there are a few errors in both spelling and word formation (spelled/spelt), it is easier to read and, therefore, would warrant a 6 rather than a 5.

虽然在拼写和构词方面（如 spelled、spelt）有一些错误，但它更容易阅读，所以，会得6分而不是5分。

| | Lexical Resource | 词汇多样性 |
|---|---|---|
| Level 7 | • uses a sufficient range of vocabulary to allow some flexibility and precision<br>• uses less common lexical items with some awareness of style and collocation<br>• may produce occasional errors in word choice, spelling and/or word formation | • 使用足够的词汇，体现一定灵活性及准确性<br>• 使用不常见词汇，对语体及搭配有一定认识<br>• 在选择用词、拼写和（或）构词方面可能偶尔出现错误 |

▶ **uses a sufficient range of vocabulary to allow some flexibility and precision** 使用足够的词汇，体现一定灵活性及准确性

The keywords here are '***flexibility and precision***'. If the examiner feels that he understands precisely what is meant and that the words enable him to do that, a 7 is warranted. There also should be a good range of synonyms used.

这里的关键词是"**灵活性及准确性**"。如果考官认为文章中的用词使他能精准地理解文章意思，那打7分是合理的。这里还需要有比较丰富的同义词的使用。

▶ **uses less common lexical items with some awareness of style and collocation** 使用不常见词汇，对语体及搭配有一定认识

The main differences between a 6 here are the accuracy of the 'less common' words and the fact that 'collocations' are being used. Collocations could be grouped into two main groups:

相较于6分，7分的主要区别是使用"不常见"词汇的准确性以及"词语搭配"的使用。词语搭配可分为两大类：

1. words that commonly 'go' together: for example, 'take a photo' 通常一起"出现"的单词：如 take a photo

2. words that, once they are together, give a 3rd meaning 当放在一起，会表示第三种意思的单词

For example, '***take on*** the mission'. 'Take' would generally mean 'to move / remove something', with 'on' meaning 'used to show that something is in a position above something else and touching it'. When these two words are added together, the meaning bears little relation to the individual ones.

例如，在 ***take on*** the mission 中，take 通常是指"移动或拿走某物"，on 的意思是"用来表示某物位于另一物之上并与之接触"。但当这两个词合到一起的时候，这个词组的意思与单独两个单词的意思没有关系。

▶ **may produce occasional errors in word choice, spelling and/or word formation** 在选择用词、拼写和（或）构词方面可能偶尔出现错误

**Using our example from Level 5:**

依然用5分标准说明中使用过的例子：

> *This sentence is spelt wrong on purpose, although some words are spell worse than others.*

The error in the above sentence is very subtle and could easily be missed when reading a passage quickly. It should also be understood that the majority of sentences are spelt correctly.

这个例句中的错误非常细微，在快速阅读一篇文章时很容易被忽略。并且大多数句子中的拼写是正确的。

# Chapter 4 Grammatical Range and Accuracy
## 语法多样性和准确性

Grammar is the part of any language that most people don't like, but like any test of language, it's always included. Two things are being looked at within IELTS: Range and Accuracy.

在任何语言中，语法是大多数人都不喜欢的部分。但就像任何语言测试一样，它总是包含在其中。雅思考试主要考查两个方面：多样性和准确性。

## ▶ Range 多样性

This specifies the different types of grammatical structures that you can use. It would include things like tenses, subject-verb agreements, plurals, conditionals, simple and complex sentence structures, to mention a few. It's beyond the scope of this book to teach you English Grammar, but you should learn as much as possible to reach the IELTS exam's higher scores.

这里指定你可以使用的不同类型的语法结构，包括时态、主谓一致、复数、条件句、简单句与复合句等等。语法教学不在这本书的范围内，但你应该尽可能多学一些，以拿到雅思写作更高的分数。

## ▶ Accuracy 准确性

As the name implies, this is how accurate your grammar is when writing. So, when using the different structures indicated in Range, they must be correct. The more correct sentences you can provide during the exam, the higher your score will be.

顾名思义，这是指你写作时语法的准确程度。所以，在使用不同的语法结构时，要确保它们使用正确。在写作考试中，语法准确的句子越多，你的分数就越高。

| | Grammatical Range and Accuracy | 语法多样性和准确性 |
|---|---|---|
| Level 4 | • uses only a very limited range of structures with only rare use of subordinate clauses<br>• some structures are accurate but errors predominate, and punctuation is often faulty | • 仅能使用非常有限的语法结构，只能偶尔使用从句<br>• 一些语法结构使用正确，但错误占多数，且标点符号经常出错 |

▶ **uses only a very limited range of structures** 仅能使用非常有限的语法结构

A range of structures may include different tenses or different styles of sentences. Level 4 means that this range is very small, so most of the sentences follow the same structure.

一系列的语法结构可能包括不同的时态或句式。在 **4** 分的标准里，语法结构非常单一，大多数句子都使用相同结构。

▶ **... with only rare use of subordinate clauses** 只能偶尔使用从句

This means that independent/subordinate clauses are only used a couple/few times in the whole text. An example of a sentence with a subordinate clause:

这意味着独立或从属从句在整篇文章中只使用了几次。下面是使用一个从句的例子：

**· Example ·**

*When I read books, I like reading Sci-Fi.*

▶ **some structures are accurate but errors predominate** 一些语法结构使用正确，但错误占多数

This means exactly what it says. That some of the sentences are correct, but most of them aren't.

正如字面意思。有些句子的语法是正确的，但大多数是错误的。

▶ **... and punctuation is often faulty** 且标点符号经常出错

'Punctuation' refers to things like full stops '.', or commas ',' and many others. So if you often don't end sentences correctly, a 4 will be given.

"标点符号"是指如句号（ . ）、逗号（ , ）和其他符号。所以如果你经常在作文句尾处不能使用正确的标点符号，这一项只能得 **4** 分。

| | Grammatical Range and Accuracy | 语法多样性和准确性 |
|---|---|---|
| Level 5 | • uses only a limited range of structures<br>• attempts complex sentences but these tend to be less accurate than simple sentences<br>• may make frequent grammatical errors and punctuation may be faulty; errors can cause some difficulty for the reader | • 仅能使用有限的语法结构<br>• 试图使用复杂句，但复杂句的准确性通常不及简单句的准确性<br>• 可能经常出现语法及标点符号使用的错误；这些错误会对读者造成一定的阅读困难 |

▶ **uses only a limited range of structures 仅能使用有限的语法结构**

This means that only a few different types of sentence structure are used in the text that the candidate has written.

这里指在作文中仅使用了几种不同的句子结构。

▶ **attempts complex sentences but these tend to be less accurate than simple sentences 试图使用复杂句，但复杂句的准确性通常不及简单句的准确性**

Here the criterion describes the use of complex structures in the text. Simple sentences may be accurate, but complex ones have errors in them. Complex structures would quite often contain words like: who, what, when, where, why and how in order to establish subordinate clauses, but they can also include elements like conditionals, not only...but also, etc. For a 5, although the text does indeed contain complex structures these are mostly incorrect.

这里的标准描述的是在作文中复杂句式的使用。作文中的简单句可能是准确的，但复杂句有错误。复杂句的结构通常会包含这些词，如 who、what、when、where、why 和 how，来构成从句。但也可能会包含元素，如条件句 not only ..., but also ... 等等。在 5 分标准里，虽然作文中包含了复杂句，但大多是不正确的。

▶ **may make frequent grammatical errors and punctuation may be faulty; errors can cause some difficulty for the reader 可能经常出现语法及标点符号使用的错误；这些错误会对读者造成一定的阅读困难**

There is no number that can be attached to 'frequent', it will be up to the examiner. For me, I believe that 'frequent' would be more than half of the sentences written. The advice here would be similar to that of Lexical Resource 5; if it needs to read it twice, it is causing the examiner some difficulty.

对于"经常出现"没有一个可量化的数字标准，这取决于考官。对我来说，我认为"经常出现"应该是指作文中超过一半的句子。在这里，我的建议与 5 分的词汇多样性标准比较相似。如果需要读两遍，就是给考官带来了阅读困难。

*Yesterday, we will together be gone swimming*

Not only are there errors in tenses here, but also word order. It's not particularly difficult to figure out what is meant, but it will take a little time. Also, note the lack of a full stop at the end of the sentence. That would be considered a punctuation fault.

这里不仅时态有误，而且词序也有错误。要弄明白这句话的意思并不难，但需要一点时间。另外，注意句尾没有句号。这会被视为标点符号的错用。

*Important Information: Punctuation can be particularly tricky as it may vary between writers. The biggest elements of punctuation that examiners will look out for are Capital letters appearing where they shouldn't and missing full stops. These days another issue that is being discussed is spacing after a comma or full stop when the text has been typed rather than written. If there are some with spaces and some not, that is a potential signal of a larger problem and the examiner may reduce your mark because of it.*

**重要信息**：标点符号算是比较棘手的问题，因为不同的作者有不同的使用方式。考官最关注的是，字母在不该大写的时候大写，以及句尾没有句号。最近讨论的另一个问题是，当文本是打字而不是书写时，关于逗号或句号后的空格。如果有些有空格，有些没有，这是一个出现大问题的潜在信号，考官可能会因此而扣分。

| | Grammatical Range and Accuracy | 语法多样性和准确性 |
|---|---|---|
| Level 6 | •uses a mix of simple and complex sentence forms<br>•makes some errors in grammar and punctuation but they rarely reduce communication | •综合使用简单句式与复杂句式<br>•在语法及标点符号方面有一些错误，但这些错误很少影响交流 |

▶ **uses a mix of simple and complex sentence forms** 综合使用简单句式与复杂句式

This element really speaks for itself. Like other elements, there isn't a number that needs to be reached to indicate a mix. Experienced examiners will generally consider a mix as around the 40-50% mark.

这一项标准不言自明。如同其他元素，没有一个可量化的数字来表明句式综合的程度。经验丰富的考官会把综合使用句式作为 **40%–50%** 的打分比重。

*Tiny Tip:* *This can be challenging in Task 1, as it's perfectly possible for candidates to write only a very few (complex) sentences (6 or 7), but by doing so, they would normally not be writing using simple structures and aiming for 7 or more.*

**小提示：** 对于 Task 1，这会比较有挑战性。因为考生很可能只能写几句话（6 句或 7 句），通常这种情况下就不会用简单句来写作，而是写更多的复杂句，但也会更有可能得到 7 分甚至更高的分数。

▶ **makes some errors in grammar and punctuation but they rarely reduce communication** 在语法及标点符号方面有一些错误，但这些错误很少影响交流

Here, again, we would refer you to the same concept as in the Lexical Resource. If it's a little wrong but you don't need to read it twice, then a 6 can be given. If examiners read it twice, then that could be classed as 'some' difficulty and examiners will look carefully at whether it should be a 5. Using our example from Grammar and Accuracy Level 5:

同样，我建议你去查看词汇多样性部分的标准。如果只出现一点错误，不需要考官阅读两次，就会得 6 分。但如果考官需要阅读两次，那就会被视为作文会造成"一定的"阅读困难，考官会仔细查看并考虑给 5 分。把在 5 分语法与准确性的标准出现的例子用在这里，则是：

> *Today, we will together go swimming*

Here the sentence is more correct than previously and although the word order is wrong (and there's still no full stop), it doesn't stop us from easily understanding what is meant.

这个例句比之前的准确性更高，虽然词序仍然是错误的，而且句尾没有句号，但这并不影响读者轻松明白句子的意思。

| | Grammatical Range and Accuracy | 语法多样性和准确性 |
|---|---|---|
| Level 7 | •uses a variety of complex structures<br>•produces frequent error-free sentences<br>•has good control of grammar and punctuation but may make a few errors | •运用各种复杂的语法结构<br>•多数句子准确无误<br>•对语法及标点符号掌握较好，但有时出现少许错误 |

### ▶ uses a variety of complex structures 运用各种复杂的语法结构

Like other criterion, there isn't a number that examiners can use to quantify a 'variety', they must simply use good judgement. But I would expect a number of compound, complex and compound-complex sentences of different structures.

正如其他标准，考官无法用数字量化"各种"，即多样性，所以他们必须只能主观判断。但我会希望读到一些复合词、复合句和不同结构的复合复句。

### ▶ produces frequent error-free sentences 多数句子准确无误

Again, there isn't a definite number but, experienced examiners generally believe that 66% or more of completely error-free sentences to give a 7.

同样，这里没有确切的数字来量化。但经验丰富的考官通常认为，作文中如果66%或更多的句子准确无误的话可以打7分。

### ▶ has good control of grammar and punctuation but may make a few errors 对语法及标点符号掌握较好，但有时出现少许错误

For many examiners 'a few errors' is quite difficult to judge, it generally comes with experience. Using the above figure as a guide, you could expect to have 34% or fewer errors for this element.

对很多考官来说，"少许错误"非常难判断，通常需要经验。用上面的数据作为指导，如果出现少于34%的错误就可以达到这个标准。

Well done for getting through this first section of the book. This is the end of Section 1 of this book. I hope that now you have a good understanding of the Writing Criteria used by the examiners. Like I said during the introduction, I firmly believe that simply by understanding what the examiners are looking for, you can fully understand what parts of the English language you can concentrate on to increase your score and hopefully obtain the level you need.

非常棒，你已经完成了本书的 Section 1，现在已经到了 Section 1 的结尾。我希望你现在已经能很好地理解考官的评分标准。正如我在前言中所说，我坚信，只要了解考官在找什么，你就能充分了解你可以通过专注于英语语言的哪些部分来提高你的分数，并有希望获得你需要的分数。

Simply reading this book once will NOT be sufficient. English must be studied and used daily to improve. There's an English saying, 'If you don't use it, you lose it.' It means that if you don't constantly use and practice something, in this case, English, you will forget how to use/write it.

仅仅把这本书读一遍是不够的，必须每天学习和使用英语才能提高。有句英语谚语说："如果你不用它，你就会失去它。"因此，如果你不经常使用和练习英语，你就会忘记如何使用或写英语。

Learning a language is a process that takes time and should be adequately planned. I wouldn't advise waiting until the last minute to cram for an IELTS exam. It's incredibly difficult to raise your score by 1 or 2 points in a matter of weeks. Even if you succeeded in doing that, you would find it challenging during your studies on your arrival at university.

学习语言是一个需要时间、充分准备的过程。我不建议等到最后一刻才临时准备雅思考试。在几周内将你的分数提高 1-2 分非常困难。即使你成功了，你也会发现进入大学后，你的学习过程充满挑战。

The information I have given you in this part has helped many of my past students increase their scores and feel more confident when taking the IELTS Writing exam because they understand more about how it works from the examiner's point of view rather than the candidate's.

这一部分分享的信息已经帮助我的许多学生提高了分数，让他们在参加雅思写作考试时更加自信，因为他们能更多地从考官的角度而不是考生的角度理解评分标准。

Overall, just remember that examiners are human beings and have a job to do. If you give them the language and elements necessary for a Level 7, that's what they'll give you; if not, they won't. It's nothing personal; it's just that's what they believe they should give you according to the criteria.

总的来说，你要记住考官也是主观个体，评分是他们的工作。如果你的语言和标准达到了 7 分所要求的，他们就会给你 7 分；如果达不到，他们就不会给。这不是针对你，只是他们认为应该根据标准给你对应的分数。

# Section II

# Task 1 Preparation and Question Types

# Task 1 备考及问题类型

In this section, I will provide examples of Task 1 topics that may appear in the IELTS Writing exam. Please DO NOT just blindly memorise these answers. Look at them, learn any unfamiliar words and how to use them, and understand why I'm using those words or the grammar structures to create your answers for the exam.

在这一部分，我将提供一些可能出现在雅思写作考试 Task 1中的话题及例文。但请不要只是盲目地背答案。仔细看例文，学习任何不熟悉的词及如何使用它们，再去理解为什么我会用这些词和语法结构，进而写出你自己的作文。

*Disclaimer:* *The answers I've written are provided as examples of the different scores based on the information given in the Public IELTS Writing criteria. They do not guarantee that anyone would achieve those scores in a real IELTS exam and should be taken as guidelines only. It should also be understood that the marks given by examiners are for the task as a whole, not the individual paragraphs or sentences.*

**免责声明：** 本书中不同分数的答案范例的依据标准是公众版雅思写作评分标准。这些答案不能保证任何人在实际的雅思考试中取得相应的分数，在此仅供参考。同时需要清楚，考官在写作考试中是给文章整体打分，而不是每个部分单独打分。

# Chapter 1 Task 1 Preparation
## Task 1 备考

## ■ Question Types and Different Approaches

All approaches should include an Introduction, Middle and End, and the Introduction should always have the same information. It should rephrase/reword the chart title and include information about the axes of the chart or the column and row headings of the table. It should also include any headings given about the data provided. The Middle or 'Body' of the text should be split into 2, or very occasionally 3, paragraphs and will contain all the details of whatever you're referring to. The End or 'Summary' should be just that, an overall statement of the information.

所有的作文内容都需要包含开头、中间主体部分以及结尾，而且开头内容基本一致。这需要换一个词或短语描述图表标题，同时包含图表的坐标轴信息，或者表格的行标题和列标题，也要包括所提供的数据的标题。作文的主体部分通常分为两段，偶尔会分为三段，并且要包含你所提及内容的所有细节。结尾段或"总结"段，就是对所有信息的一个整体陈述。

As mentioned earlier, Task 1 is all about comparing and summarising; therefore, when first looking at a graph or graphs, you need to understand the data you are looking at and how you can organise it. This is perhaps the most challenging part of Task 1, but also the most important. You shouldn't just list the data you can see, but show the examiner that you can group data items together and then show them that you understand the meaning behind the data. When it comes to the final paragraph, the Summary, this understanding is crucial. Ask yourself the question – **What does all this mean?** For a graph, maybe some elements have increased or decreased over time. For a map, it may mean that things are easier to access or that there is more of something, housing, for example, which in turn means that more people can live there.

如前所述，**Task 1**是关于比较和总结。因此，当第一眼看到图表时，你需要先理解所看到的数据，并思考如何在作文中组织这些数据。这可能是 **Task 1**里最有挑战的部分，但也是最重要的部分。不能只是将看到的数据列出来，而是需要向考官展示你可以将数据进行组合，并且证明你理解数据背后的含义。**Task 1**的总结段很关键，更能显示出你对数据的理解程度。问问自己这个问题：**这些数据代表了什么？**对于图表题来说，可能是在某一段时间内有些元素的上涨或下降。在地图题中，可能代表有些区域更方便进入或者某些事物增多。例如，如果地图上出现更多房子，则意味着更多人可以住在那里。

The following styles of questions and the different approaches I have explained are those that I have found helpful in selecting and comparing data and understanding where I should put them with the framework of Task 1. I haven't written example answers for these. They're simply for you to understand how to look at the different questions and think about how to structure your essay appropriately.

以下列出的不同形式的问题及写作思路是我认为在 Task 1 中将数据进行选择和比较时非常有帮助的。我并没有写相应的范文。只是让你理解如何审题以及以合适的方式安排作文结构。

Something to consider when writing Task 1 is that in Paragraph 1 (P1), you will simply describe the data, and this may be in the Present or Past tenses (depending on the data), but Paragraph 2 (P2) will not only just explain the data, it should also compare it to P1. Don't forget: within the question, you should 'make comparisons where relevant' as written in the Task instructions. That's the fundamentals of most maps, graphs and tables – comparative data.

写 Task 1 时需要考虑的是，在第一段中，你只需要简单地描述数据，可以用现在时或过去时（取决于数据）。但第二段不仅要解释数据，还应该与第一段进行比较。不要忘记：在题目中，一般会要求考生"在相关的地方进行比较"。这是大多数地图题、图表题和表格题的基础——比较数据。

*Important Tip:* *I would suggest 30-40 words for both the Introduction and Summary (60-80 in total), and then 40-50 words in each of the two paragraphs (80-100 in total). This looks more pleasing to the eye, as it is quite balanced and gives you a target to achieve for each section that, with practice, is reasonably easy to reach and means that you don't need to check your Word Count unless absolutely necessary.*

**重要提示：** 我建议 Task 1 的开头段和结尾段各写 30–40 字（共计 60–80 字），两个主体段落每段各写 40–50 字（共计 80–100 字）。这样看起来更舒服，因为内容分布平衡，并且你会更清晰每个部分的目标，通过练习是比较容易达成的，这也意味着除非特别必要，否则你不需要检查字数。

# ■ Task 1 (Academic)

## ▶ Type 1: One Graph/Table (1G/T)    一张图表或表格（1G/T）

This answer style is perhaps the easiest of them all and should be used as a foundation for **ALL** of the other types, including those of Maps and Processes.

这种题型的答案可能是所有题型中最简单的，应该作为**所有**其他类型（包括地图题和流程图题）的基础。

Typical Framework: Introduction, 2 Main Body Paragraphs, Summary.

典型的作文结构：开头段、主体段 2 段、总结段。

The first thing you need to do here is to group the different data into related areas that can go into either the first or second paragraphs in your text.

你需要做的第一件事，就是将不同的数据根据作文的布局需要进行分组，有的数据放在主体段第 1 段，有的放在主体段第 2 段。

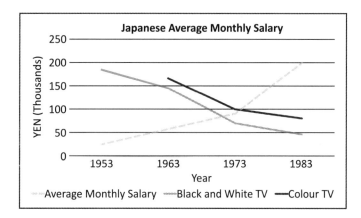

For example, in the above graph, you can see three separate data streams: Average Monthly Salary, Black and White TV and Colour TV, with the y-axis showing amounts in YEN and the x-axis showing four different years.

例如，在上面这张图表中，你可以看到三条独立的数据：平均月薪、黑白电视和彩色电视，竖轴代表日元的金额，横轴显示了四个不同的年份。

There are several different ways to group this data; I've listed two of the more logical ones below:

有几种不同的方式对这些数据进行分组，我在下面列出了两个比较符合逻辑的分组方式：

Group 1: Black and White TV, Colour TV    分组 1：黑白电视、彩色电视
Group 2: Average Monthly Salary    分组 2：平均月薪
Or 或者

Group 1: **1953, 1963**　分组 1：1953、1963

Group 2: **1973, 1983**　分组 2：1973、1983

At this point, once you've decided which grouping you want to use, you can then determine what data you are going to include and then compare. Using the graph shown, if I were writing an answer, the first paragraph would consist of the data about the TVs with some comparisons. I'd describe the Average Salary in paragraph two and make some further comparisons. In the summary, I'd simply put that the Average Salary is going up and the price of TVs are going down.

现在，一旦你决定要使用哪个分组，就可以确定要包含哪些数据，然后进行比较。如上面所示的图表，如果我来写作文，在主体段的第 1 段中，会包括关于电视的数据和一些比较。我会在主体段第 2 段中描述平均月薪，并进行进一步比较。在总结段里，我会简单地说明平均月薪在上涨，电视价格在下降。

▶ **Type 2:Two Graphs/Tables (2G/T)　两张图表或表格（2G/T）**

Typical Framework: Introduction, 2 Main Body Paragraphs, Summary.

典型结构：开头段、主体段 2 段、总结段。

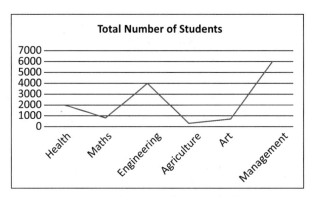

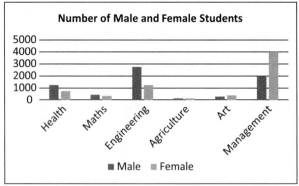

This type of question is basically the same as the previous one. With two charts or tables, however, it makes the grouping much easier. In Paragraph 1, you can describe the data in Chart 1; in Paragraph 2, you can explain what's in Chart 2. You can then further break down the data into two halves for each paragraph. Health, Maths and Engineering for the first half and Agriculture, Art and Management for the second.

这类题型和前一个题型基本相同。但是，因为有两张图表或表格，数据分组就更容易了。你可以在主体段第1段里描述图表1的数据，在主体段第2段里描述图表2的数据。然后你可以进一步将每个段落的数据分成两部分。在每段前半部分分析健康、数学和工程专业的数据，在每段后半部分分析农业、艺术以及管理专业的数据。

The comparisons can be made in each individual paragraph, with the summary describing the data from both charts. An example of the summary is shown below.

每个图表的数据比较可以在每一个主体段内分别进行，在总结段里可以整体描述两张图表的数据。下面就是总结段的示例。

_Summary Idea:_ _The fact that Health, Engineering and Management are much more popular than Maths, Agriculture and Art. Or maybe that the only course where girls outnumber boys is Management._

_Important Tip:_ _Don't forget to not just list the data in each paragraph. Otherwise, the Task Achievement score won't be very high._

**重要提示：**一定记住，每个段落里不能只罗列数据。否则，作文的分数不会很高。

▶ **Type 3:Three Graphs/Tables (3G/T)**    三张图表或表格（3G/T）

Typical Framework: Introduction, 3 Main Body Paragraphs, Summary.

典型结构：开头段、主体段3段、总结段。

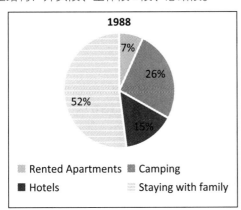

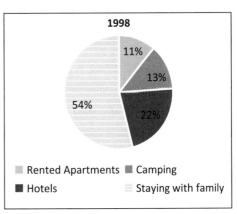

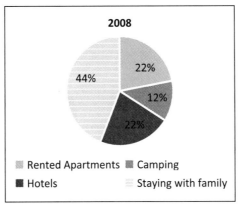

With three graphs, not necessarily of the same type as shown above, it still builds on the previous type. It must be remembered that although having a total of 4 paragraphs is typical, it is not compulsory. So, an option of having three paragraphs in the body of your text would be called for here.

三张图表的题型，图表形式不一定跟例图一样，但仍然建立在之前题型的基础上。必须记住虽然这种题型写成4段比较常见，但这并不是必需的。所以，在这里你的作文主体段可以是3段，再加上1段开头段和1段结尾段，一共是5段。

*Tiny Tip:* *It would also be possible/logical to split the types of accommodation into two groups/paragraphs and then talk about the three different years in each paragraph.*

**小提示：** 如果将住宿的不同类型分成两段写，然后在每一段同时讨论三个不同的年份也是合乎逻辑的。这样主体段就是2段。

The comparisons can be made in each individual paragraph, with the summary describing the data from all the charts. An example of the summary is shown below.

对数据的对比可以在每个段落分别进行，在总结段中描述图表的整体数据情况。下面就是总结段的示例。

*Summary Idea:* *The fact that 'Staying with Family' has always been the largest value.*

*Tiny Tip:* *If you had four charts, it would be easier to return to the previous structure type and have two groups of 2.*

**小提示：** 如果题目中有四张图表，那么使用之前提到的结构，即主体段2段，每段各分析两张图表数据的方法会更加容易。

### ▶ Type 4: A Mix of a Graph and a Table (1GT)　混合图表与表格（1GT）

Typical Framework: Introduction, 2 Main Body Paragraphs, Summary.

典型结构：开头段、主体段2段、总结段。

| Total value of fish imports to the US in $bn | |
| --- | --- |
| 2008 | 6.85 |
| 2012 | 7.8 |

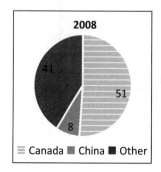

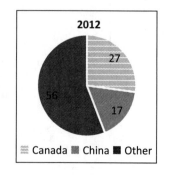

*This has been adapted from the question that appears later in this book.

*改编自本书后面出现的一道题。

This type of layout can be treated as the same as 2G/T (2 Graphs/Tables). The first paragraph will describe the table, and the second paragraph will represent the pie charts. You could also approach this from a yearly perspective and have 2008 data in Paragraph 1 and 2012 data in Paragraph 2, but it seems, to me, unnecessarily complicated.

这种题型的作文布局和两张图表或表格的题型一样。主体段第1段描述表格，主体段第2段展示饼图的数据。你也可以从年份的角度来分析，主体段第1段分析2008年的数据，主体段第2段描述2012年的数据，但这个角度对我来说是复杂且没有必要的。

One potential problem you may encounter is that you can't write enough words to reach the 150-word minimum. This could certainly be the case as the table, and therefore Paragraph 1, would be very short. There are a couple of ways of dealing with an issue like this:

你可能会遇到的一个潜在问题是，达不到最低字数要求，即150字。原因可能是表格里的数据比较少，导致主体段第1段比较短。有两个方法可以解决这个问题：

1. Create some extra data that you can use from the charts. 从饼图中找出更多的数据进行分析。

2. Expand the summary to include ideas that you have. 扩展总结段，加上自己的一些想法。

With the first idea, it would be straightforward to calculate that the total value of Canada's imports is valued at around $3.5bn (51% of 6.85bn). You could calculate the other figures if you're pretty good at numeracy/maths.

如果是第一种方法，可以直接计算出从加拿大进口的价值总额约为35亿美元（在所有进口总额68.5亿美元中占比51%）。如果你的数学计算能力很好，也可以计算出其他的数据。

Expanding the summary would also gain you a few words, just be careful not to start repeating the data. I'd suggest summarising the table and the pie charts separately rather than combining them. An example of the extended summary is shown below.

扩展总结段也会使你多写一些单词，但是要注意不要重复罗列数据。我建议将表格和饼图中的数据分开总结，要比合起来总结更好。下面就是扩展总结段的示例。

**Extended Summary Example:** *To summarise all the information then, it is very clear that the value of fish imports has increased overall by a considerable amount. In addition to this, China's piece of the pie has also more than doubled in the timescale given. (41 words)*

▶ **Type 5: Two Maps (2M)**　两张地图题（2M）

Typical Framework: Introduction, 2 Main Body Paragraphs, Summary.

典型结构：开头段、主体段2段、总结段。

**The office building now**

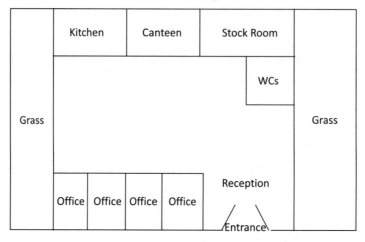

**Planned development**

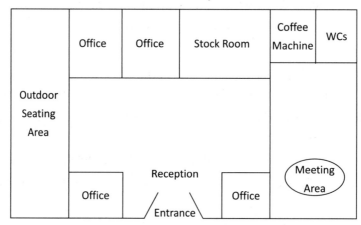

This type of question is very similar to 2G/T (2 Graphs/Tables). In Paragraph 1, you can describe the picture in Map 1; in Paragraph 2, you can explain what's different in Map 2.

这类题型跟两张图表或表格非常相似。在主体段第1段，你可以描述地图1，并在主体段第2段描述地图2的不同之处。

The comparisons can be made in each individual paragraph, with the summary describing the data from both maps. An example of the summary is shown below.

每一个段落都可以对地图进行比较，并在总结段整体描述两张图的数据。下面就是总结段的示例。

*Summary Idea:* *The fact that availability of cooked food doesn't seem to be important to the management of this office.*

*Tiny Tip:* *Remember to keep to the same order of description. So, if you started with Entrance and Reception in Paragraph 1; start there in Paragraph 2 too.*

**小提示：** 记住描述地图时的顺序要保持一致。所以，如果在主体段第1段里，你是从入口和接待处开始描述地图，那在主体段第2段时也从这里开始。

# ▶ Type 6: Processes (1P) 流程图题（1P）

Typical Framework: Introduction, 2 Main Body Paragraphs, Summary.

典型结构：开头段、主体段2段、总结段。

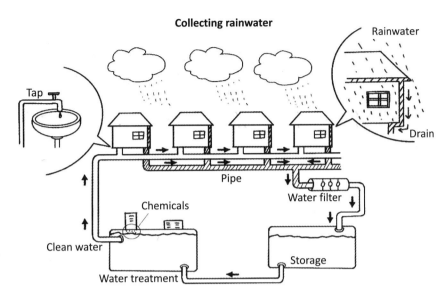

**Collecting rainwater**

Perhaps the most challenging part of a process, certainly if it's not numbered like the diagram shown above, is to divide it into two and choose the information you want to put into each paragraph. Sometimes it's self-evident where you can divide it. For example, if there are ten processes, an easy way could be to describe the first five in paragraph one and the next five in paragraph two.

因为不像图表题中有明确的数字，流程图题最有挑战性的部分可能是考虑如何将图上的信息分成两部分，并选择你想放到每段的信息。有时你可以在哪儿分段很明显。例如，如果有10个流程，最简单的方法就是在主体段第1段里写5个流程，主体段第2段写另外5个流程。

The above example, though, is a little more complicated. My preferred way of splitting it would be 'above' and 'below' ground. This means that the first paragraph will be relatively short, with the second being longer, but to me, at least, it seems logical. So, P1 would include the rainwater collection, whereas P2 would consist of the filtering, storage, treatment, and delivery to the tap.

不过例图稍微有些复杂。我比较倾向把它分为"地上"和"地下"两部分。这也说明，主体段第1段会相对较短，主体段第2段较长。但至少对我来说，这样安排比较合乎逻辑。因此，主体段第1段会描述雨水收集的步骤，主体段第2段会包括过滤、存储、处理和输送到水龙头。

*Summary Example:* *In summary then, it seems that turning rainwater into water that we can use indoors is a relatively straightforward process with the correct equipment.*

*Tiny Tip:* *For the example above, it would be possible to have a structure of: Introduction, 1 Paragraph, Summary.*

**小提示：** 对于上面给出的流程图，也可以尝试另一种结构：开头段、主体段1段、总结段。

## ■ Task 1 (General)

Typical Framework: Appropriate Salutation, 3 Main Body Paragraphs, Appropriate Closing.
典型结构：恰当的称呼、主体段3段、恰当的结束语。

Your company sent you to complete a course in another country. You have lost the certificate received at the end of the course. Write a letter to the principal of the college where you took the course. In your letter:

• *Tell them how you lost the certificate*

• *Explain why you need it now*

• *Say what action you would like them to take.*

The challenge with the General Writing task is truly understanding the situation, then choosing the formality you should use and, therefore, what opening and closing you should have.
培训类写作的难点是要真正理解题目的情境，并选择书信的正式程度，以及如何恰当地开头和结尾。

Below is a table explaining the correct choices of a letter's openings and closings.
下面的表格解释了书信开头和结尾的正确选择 。

| | Opening 开头 | Closing 结尾 |
| --- | --- | --- |
| Formal 正式用语 | Dear Sir/Madam, | Yours faithfully, |
| Semi-Formal 半正式用语 | Dear Mr. Foster, | Yours sincerely, |
| Informal 非正式用语 | Dear James, | Yours/Kind regards/With thanks etc. |

In the example question shown, you are a student and must write to the college principal. With this kind of relationship, plus the fact that we are not given the principal's name, I would choose the Formal type of letter. Each paragraph would then cover one of the details listed in the instructions, and finally, close the letter with the above mentioned endings.
在上面的例题中，你是一名学生并且要给大学校长写一封信。基于这种关系，再加上我们不知道校长的名字，我会选择写正式类型的信。然后，每一段将涵盖题目中列出的一个细节，最后以表格中所列的正式用语结尾。

**Tiny Tip:** *If you're not sure about the level of formality to choose, I would suggest you choose Semiformal or Formal, as the only time you would need informal is if you're writing to someone you know well, like a friend or a parent. EVERYTHING else, would be formal or semi.*

**小提示：**如果你不确定选择哪种正式程度，我建议你选择半正式或正式，因为你只有在给很熟悉的人，比如朋友或父母写信的时候才会是非正式的。其余时候，基本都是使用正式或半正式用语写信。

**Important Information:** *Sometimes, the full salutation is given to you in the question. For example: 'Dear Sir or Madam'. This means that it's easy to decide on the level of formality.*

**重要信息：**有的时候，题目中会提供完整称呼语，例如：Dear Sir or Madam。这样你会更容易决定书信的正式程度。

# Chapter 2 Question Types and Sample Answers
## 题目类型及答案范例

## ■ Charts

Example 1 *Question and Answer*

*You should spend about 20 minutes on this task.*

> **The charts below give information about the percentage of volunteers working for different organisations in one country in 2008 and 2014.**
>
> **Summarise the information by selecting and reporting the main features, and make comparisons where relevant.**

*Write at least 150 words.*

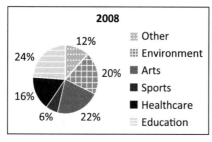
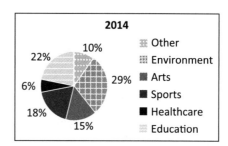

There are two pie charts that show different types of organisation's volunteers in two different years, 2008 and 2014. The organisations include Education, Healthcare, Sports, Arts, Environment and Other.

Looking firstly at the 2008 figures, it can be clearly seen that Education, Arts and Environment are the most significant sections with 24 per cent, 22 per cent and 20 per cent respectively, while Healthcare and Other show 16 per cent and 12 per cent. The smallest segment is Sports, with a mere 6 per cent.

Moving onto the 2014 chart, while Education and Arts shrank by 2 per cent and 7 per cent, Environment grew to 29 per cent. Sports expanded as well to 18 per cent, which left 10 per cent for Other and only 6 per cent for Healthcare, a reduction of 2 per cent and a whopping 10 per cent.

In summary, we can see that the figures shown changed considerably over the six years, with Sports gaining the most and Healthcare taking the biggest hit.

***Word Count: 169***

两张饼图显示了2008年和2014年这两个不同年份中不同类型组织的志愿者情况。这些组织包括：教育组织、医疗保健组织、体育组织、艺术组织、环境组织和其他组织。

先看2008年饼图中的数据，可以清楚地看到，教育组织、艺术组织和环境组织的志愿者人数占比最大，分别为24%、22%和20%，而医疗保健组织和其他组织的志愿者人数占比分别为16%和12%。体育组织的志愿者人数占比最小，仅为6%。

再看2014年饼图，教育组织和艺术组织的志愿者人数占比分别缩减了2%和7%，而环境组织的志愿者人数占比增长至29%。体育组织的志愿者人数占比也增加至18%，而其他组织的志愿者人数占比减少了2%，达到10%。医疗保健组织的志愿者人数占比大幅减少了10%，仅有6%。

总之，我们可以看到，所示数据在6年中发生了相当大的变化。体育组织的志愿者人数增长最快，医疗保健组织的志愿者人数受到的影响最大。

## Example 1　*Approach*

2G/T is the most logical here.

这种作文格式最适合两张图表或表格的题型。

- Paragraph 1 – Pie Chart 1 – Biggest, Smallest

  主体段1——饼图1——最大的数据、最小的数据

- Paragraph 2 – Pie Chart 2 – Comparison of P1 Data

  主体段2——饼图2——与主体段1的数据进行比较

| Examiner's Comment | | | |
|---|---|---|---|
| Coherence and Cohesion | Logical | ☑ | |
| | Progression | Looking firstly at, Moving onto, In summary | ☑ |
| Lexical Resource | Range | ☑ | |
| | Less Common | shrank, whopping, biggest hit | ☑ |
| Grammatical Range and Accuracy | Simple Structures | ☑ | |
| | Complex Structures | ☑ | |

Example 2 *Question and Answer*

*You should spend about 20 minutes on this task.*

> **The charts below show the number and percentage of the sales of new cars in Australia in April 1994, 2004 and 2014.**
>
> **Summarise the information by selecting and reporting the main features, and make comparisons where relevant.**

*Write at least 150 words.*

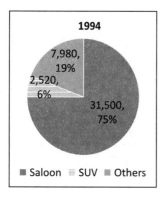
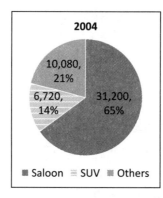
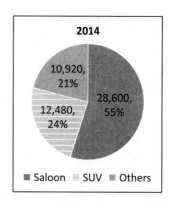

The pie charts that have been supplied illustrate sales of different types of new cars in Australia covering three distinct time frames: 1994, 2004 and 2014. Three different groups of vehicles are given: Saloon, SUV (Sports Utility Vehicle), and 'Other'.

Beginning with Saloon cars, it is evident to see that they completely dominated the market in 1994 with 75% of all car sales. However, this dropped by 10% in 2004 and a further 10% in 2014 to stand at a little over half of all Australian car sales, 28,600, which was still dominant but significantly weaker.

Moving onto SUVs and 'Others', the SUVs that have eaten into the Saloon market share the most. Beginning in 1994, with a mere 6%, this more than doubled in 2004, reaching 14%, and then nearly doubled again, to 24%. Although 'Others' did expand by 2% to reach 21% in 2004, there was not any further improvement in 2014.

Overall, it is undeniable that SUVs have increased in popularity in Australia over these 20 years and have made significant inroads into the Saloon share of the market.

***Word Count: 182***

所提供的饼图说明了澳大利亚不同类型新车的销售情况，涵盖了3个不同时间段：1994年、2004年和2014年。图中给出了3类不同车辆的数据：轿车、SUV（运动型多功能汽车）和其他汽车。

首先看看轿车的销量情况。显然，1994年，轿车以拥有汽车总销量75%的份额完全占据市场主导地位。但该比例在2004年下降了10%，2014年又下降了10%，占澳大利亚汽车总销量的一半多一点：28,600，轿车虽然仍占据市场主导地位，但明显减弱。

再看看SUV和其他汽车的销量情况。SUV的销量占据了轿车市场销量的最大份额。从1994年开始，该比例只有6%，到2004年翻了一倍多，达到14%，之后又翻了差不多一倍，达到24%。虽然在2004年，其他汽车的销量增长了2%，达到21%，但在2014年无进一步提高。

总体而言，在过去的20年里，SUV在澳大利亚越来越受欢迎，其销量占据轿车市场销量的份额有显著提升，这一点不可否认。

## Example 2  *Approach*

3G/T is the most logical here. I've deliberately divided the structure into data rather than the number of charts as 'Saloon' data is so dominant.

这种作文格式最适合三张图表或表格的题型。因为轿车的数据占主导地位，所以这里我有意用数据来划分文章段落，而不是每张图表作为一个段落。

- Paragraph 1 – Pie Chart 1, 2, 3 – Saloon

  主体段1——饼图1、2、3——轿车

- Paragraph 2 – Pie Chart 1, 2, 3 – SUV and Others compared to Saloon

  主体段2——饼图1、2、3——SUV和其他汽车与轿车进行比较

| | | Examiner's Comment | |
|---|---|---|---|
| Coherence and Cohesion | Logical | ☑ | |
| | Progression | Beginning with, Moving onto, Overall | ☑ |
| Lexical Resource | Range | doubled, increased | ☑ |
| | Less Common | illustrate, distinct, dominant, significant | ☑ |
| Grammatical Range and Accuracy | Simple Structures | ☑ | |
| | Complex Structures | ☑ | |

Example 3 *Question and Answer*

*You should spend about 20 minutes on this task.*

> **The chart below shows the percentage of the adult population in different employment categories in one city in 2003 and 2013.**
>
> **Summarise the information by selecting and reporting the main features, and make comparisons where relevant.**

*Write at least 150 words.*

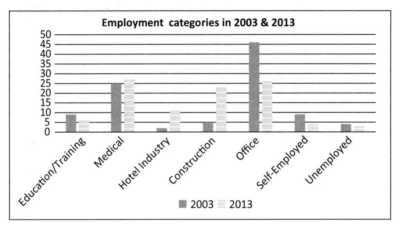

The bar chart illustrates different fields of employment that adults have in a city in two different years: 2003 and ten years later.

It can be clearly observed that there are stark differences between the two years. In 2003, Office was the largest with a little over 45%, nearly double that of the second largest – Medical, with 25%. Education/Training and the Self-Employed were significantly less being a touch under 10% each and Construction half that with 5%. The final areas, namely the Hotel Industry and Unemployment brought up the rear with about 2% and 4% respectively.

When looking at 2013, Office work had plummeted to roughly 27%, whereas Medical increased slightly to around 28%. Education and Training was another one to fall 2%-3% with the Self-Employed falling further, ending up at approximately 5%. The Construction and Hotel industries showed substantial growth, with Building expanding 5-fold and Hotel shooting up nearly 10-fold. Lastly, Unemployment was reduced to about 3%.

In summary, while some industries sharply fell, others had huge increases.

***Word Count: 170***

柱状图显示了在2003年和2013年这两个不同年份中某城市内不同行业的成人就业人数情况。

可以清楚地观察到，这两个年份之间的成人就业人数占比存在明显差异。2003年，办公室工作行业的成人就业人数占比最大，为45%多一点，几乎是成人就业人数占比第二大的医疗行业（25%）的2倍。教育或培训行业和个体户的成人就业人数占比明显均略微低于10%，建筑行业的成人就业人数占比为前者的一半，为5%。最后分析的行业是酒店行业和失业部分，其成人就业人数垫底，占比分别为约2%和4%。

再看2013年，办公室工作行业的成人就业人数占比暴跌至27%左右，而医疗行业的成人就业人数占比略微上升至28%左右。教育和培训行业的成人就业人数占比也下降2%-3%，个体户的成人就业人数占比进一步下降，最终下降了约5%。建筑行业和酒店行业的成人就业人数占比大幅增长，建筑行业的成人就业人数占比增加为5倍，酒店行业的成人就业人数占比增长为近10倍。最后，失业人数占比降至3%左右。

总之，尽管有些行业的成人就业人数占比大幅下滑，但有些行业的成人就业人数占比却大幅增长。

## Example 3 *Approach*

1G/T is the most logical here. This could be divided along the x-axis here, but it would be uneven. The logical approach here is dividing it into the two different years.

这种作文格式最适合一张图表或表格的题型。这篇作文可以按横轴分段，但这样会有些不平均。所以更符合逻辑的方式是按年份分段。

- Paragraph 1 – 2003 Data

  主体段1——2003年的数据

- Paragraph 2 – 2013 Data compared to P1

  主体段2——2013年的数据与主体段1的数据进行比较

| Examiner's Comment | | | |
|---|---|---|---|
| Coherence and Cohesion | Logical | largest, second largest | ☑ |
| | Progression | In 2003, When looking at 2013; The final areas, Lastly | ☑ |
| Lexical Resource | Range | plummeted, falling, reduced; expanding, shooting up | ☑ |
| | Less Common | illustrates, observed, substantial | ☑ |
| Grammatical Range and Accuracy | Simple Structures | ☑ | |
| | Complex Structures | ☑ | |

Example 4  *Question and Answer*

*You should spend about 20 minutes on this task.*

> **The chart below shows the percentage of homes with access to computers, the Internet and broadband Internet in the UK from 2008 to 2018.**
>
> **Summarise the information by selecting and reporting the main features, and make comparisons where relevant.**

*Write at least 150 words.*

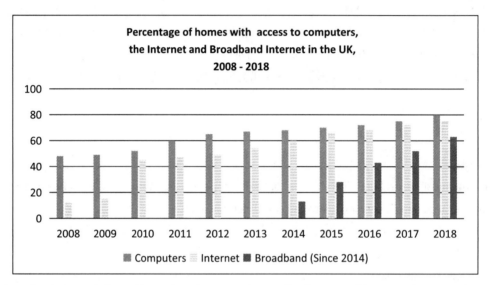

The bar chart shows information, given in percentages, the homes with access to computers, the Internet and broadband Internet over a ten-year period from 2008 to 2018. This data relates to homes that are based in UK households.

Since 2008 the figures present a steady increase in people just having access to a computer. We can see that 50% of homes had computers in 2008, and the figures rose steadily to a fraction under 80% by 2018, whereas the amount of Internet and broadband Internet users showed a quicker increase.

Standard Internet usage started off low at roughly 15% but shot up over the decade and finished off at around 75%.

The most noticeable change was in the number of broadband users, which was a late starter as it depicts that this trend started in 2014 at approximately 15% but climbed up and fell just short of regular Internet users by 2018.

Over this time frame, it is noticeable that although homes in this location had access to computers and standard Internet, it was broadband that really took off in 2014 to give people quicker Internet service.

***Word Count: 187***

柱状图显示了2008年至2018年十年间使用电脑、互联网和宽带互联网家庭的百分比信息。该数据与英国家庭相关。

自2008年以来，数据显示使用电脑的人数稳步增长。我们可以看到，2008年50%的家庭拥有电脑，到2018年，该数据稳步上升，但不到80%，而互联网和宽带互联网用户的数量增长更快。

标准互联网使用率开始时很低，约为15%，但在十年间迅速上升，最终达到75%左右。

最明显的变化是宽带用户数量，该趋势起步较晚，因为图中描述该趋势从2014年开始，宽带用户数量约为15%，但到2018年攀升至略低于常规互联网用户数量。

在这段时间内，显而易见的是，尽管英国家庭可使用电脑和标准互联网，但宽带在2014年真正迅猛发展，为人们提供更快的互联网服务。

## Example 4  *Approach*

3G/T is the most logical here. I've deliberately divided the structure into data rather than the number of charts, so I have used three paragraphs rather than the regular two.

这张图表的主体分成三段写比较符合逻辑。我有意将作文以数据分段而不是以图表数量分段，所以我在主体段用了三段而不是常见的两段。

- Paragraph 1 – Computers

  主体段1——电脑

- Paragraph 2 – Internet

  主体段2——互联网

- Paragraph 3 – Broadband

  主体段3——宽带互联网

| Examiner's Comment | | | |
|---|---|---|---|
| Coherence and Cohesion | Logical | ☒ | |
| | Progression | Since 2008 | ☒ |
| Lexical Resource | Range | rose, increase, climbed up | ☑ |
| | Less Common | depicts, location, took off | ☑ |
| Grammatical Range and Accuracy | Simple Structures | ☑ | |
| | Complex Structures | ☑ | |

Example 5   *Question and Answer*

*You should spend about 20 minutes on this task.*

> **The chart below shows the participation in organised cultural activities and sports, by gender in 2013.**
>
> **Summarise the information by selecting and reporting the main features, and make comparisons where relevant.**

*Write at least 150 words.*

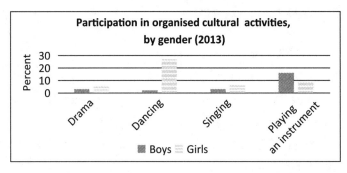

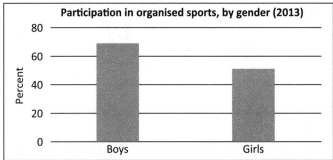

The two bar charts given show the difference in the participation of different genders as they pertain to cultural activities and sports. The year shown is 2013, and all the figures are depicted as percentages.

Firstly, when looking at the first chart, which shows various cultural activities, we can clearly see that, for the most part, the girls outstrip the boys. This is especially the case in 'Dancing', where the boy's value is a mere 2 or 3 per cent, whereas the girl's is over 25 per cent.

Moving on to the second chart, which presents sports, it offers a very different picture. Here, there are considerably more boys participating than girls. Boys are very near the 70% mark, whereas the girls register just over 50.

In summary, it is clear that the girls like participating much more than boys in the cultural events, but the opposite is true for sports.

***Word Count: 151***

所给的两张柱状图显示了不同性别人群参与文化活动和体育活动的差异。图中所示年份为2013年，所有数据均以百分比表示。

首先看第一张柱状图，该图显示了参与各种文化活动的情况。我们可以清楚地看到，在大多数情况下，参与文化活动的女孩人数超过男孩人数。在参与"舞蹈"活动方面的情况尤其如此，参与该活动的男孩人数仅为2%或3%，而参与该活动的女孩人数则超过25%。

继续看第二张柱状图，该图显示了参与体育活动的情况，这与参与文化活动的情况截然不同。在这方面，参与体育活动的男孩人数比女孩多得多。男孩人数的比例十分接近70%，而女孩人数的比例则刚刚超过50%。

总之，很明显女孩比男孩更喜欢参加文化活动，但体育活动的参与情况则正好与之相反。

## Example 5　*Approach*

2G/T is the most logical here.

这种作文格式适合两张图表或表格的题型。

● Paragraph 1 – Chart 1 – Comparisons within the chart are made by activities and sex

主体段 1——图表 1——比较活动与性别

● Paragraph 2 – Chart 2 – Compare boys to girls

主体段 2——图表 2——比较男生与女生的参与度

| Examiner's Comment | | | |
|---|---|---|---|
| Coherence and Cohesion | Logical | ☑ | |
| | Progression | Firstly, Moving on to, In summary | ☑ |
| Lexical Resource | Range | shows, presents | ☑ |
| | Less Common | pertain, outstrip | ☑ |
| Grammatical Range and Accuracy | Simple Structures | ☑ | |
| | Complex Structures | ☑ | |

Example 6 | *Question and Answer*

*You should spend about 20 minutes on this task.*

> **The table and charts below show the total value and sources of fish imports to the US between 2008 and 2017.**
>
> **Summarise the information by selecting and reporting the main features, and make comparisons where relevant.**

*Write at least 150 words.*

| Total value of fish imports to the US in $bn | |
|---|---|
| 2008 | 6.85 |
| 2012 | 7.8 |
| 2017 | 10.7 |

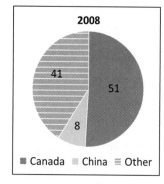
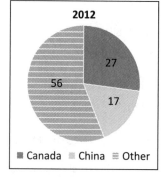
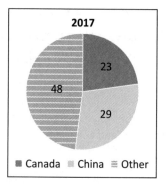

We are given information in both tabular and pie chart format, concerning the amount of fish that was imported to the USA over the decade between 2008 and 2017. The tables give us the total amount, whereas the pie charts give us locations at three different times, 2008, 2012 and 2017.

Looking firstly at the table, it is clear to see that the overall amount spent on fish increased. The figure in 2008 is $6.85 bn. In 2012, this goes up by a little less than a billion USD and then jumps a much larger step of $3 bn in 2017 to finally end up at $10.7 bn.

Moving onto the pie charts, these also change considerably. In the beginning, a little over half (51%) of all fish imports came from Canada, with 41% labelled as 'Other' and a mere 8% from China. By 2012, the Chinese portion had more than doubled (17%), Canada had fallen by a whopping 24% and 'Other' was now leading the pack with 56%. The final figures showed China growing by a further 12%, Canada shrinking again by 4%, with 'Other' now less than half.

In summary, it is evident that the US at the time bought much more fish from China than they used to.
***Word Count: 211***

我们得到了表格和饼状图形式的信息，涉及 2008 年至 2017 年十年间美国进口鱼的数量。表格给出美国进口鱼的总量，而饼状图给出在 2008 年、2012 年和 2017 年这 3 个不同年份的进口来源地。

首先来看表格，可以清楚地看到鱼的总消费额有所增加。2008 年，该数据为 68.5 亿美元。2012 年，该数字上升了近 10 亿美元，之后在 2017 年跃升 30 亿美元，最终达到 107 亿美元。

继续看饼图，其中的数字也有很大变化。起初，略超过一半（51%）的进口鱼来自加拿大，而 41% 的进口鱼来自"其他国家"，仅 8% 的进口鱼来自中国。到 2012 年，从中国进口的鱼数量占比增加了一倍多（17%），从加拿大进口的鱼数量占比大幅下降了 24%，而从"其他国家"进口的鱼数量占比以 56% 领先。最终数据显示，从中国进口的鱼数量占比进一步增长了 12%，从加拿大进口的鱼数量占比再次缩减了 4%，而从"其他国家"进口的鱼数量目前占比不足 50%。

总之，显然美国目前从中国进口的鱼数量较之过去大幅攀升。

## Example 6　*Approach*

2G/T is the most logical here.

这种作文格式适合两张图表或表格的题型。

- Paragraph 1 – Table data – Compare the totals

  主体段 1——表格数据——比较总数

- Paragraph 2 – Pie chart data – Compare the percentages of each country by year

  主体段 2——饼图数据——比较各国家每年的百分比数据

| | Examiner's Comment | | |
|---|---|---|---|
| Coherence and Cohesion | Logical | √ | |
| | Progression | Looking firstly at, Moving onto, final, In summary | √ |
| Lexical Resource | Range | increased, jumps, growing | √ |
| | Less Common | considerably, portion, whopping | √ |
| Grammatical Range and Accuracy | Simple Structures | √ | |
| | Complex Structures | √ | |

## ■ Tables

Example 1   *Question and Answer*

*You should spend about 20 minutes on this task.*

> **The two tables below show some responses of various age groups to a survey on their thoughts about their local library.**
>
> **Summarise the information by selecting and reporting the main features, and make comparisons where relevant.**

*Write at least 150 words.*

| Age Groups | Range of books | | |
| --- | --- | --- | --- |
| | Very good | Satisfactory | Not good |
| Under 15 | 55% | 33% | 12% |
| 15-39 | 27% | 48% | 25% |
| 40 and above | 28% | 50% | 22% |

| Age Groups | Non-Print materials (e.g. computer software and DVDs) | | | |
| --- | --- | --- | --- | --- |
| | Very good | Satisfactory | Not good | No Comment |
| Under 15 | 25% | 23% | 52% | 0% |
| 15-39 | 49% | 30% | 19% | 2% |
| 40 and above | 11% | 19% | 22% | 48% |

There are two tables given that show results of a survey about residents local library. Each table is divided by different age groups, with the first showing data about the range of books and the second showing 'Non-Print Materials'.

Looking in more detail at the first table, 'Range of books', it is clear to see that different age groups have vastly different ideas of what constitutes 'Very Good', 'Satisfactory', and 'Not Good'. 55% of under 15-year-olds thought the range was 'Very Good', which is roughly twice that of the other two groups (15-39 and 40 and above). The highest percentage for the other two groups was 'Satisfactory', with 48% and 50% respectively.

Moving on to the second table, 'Non-Print Materials', it is again apparent that there are vast differences of opinion. The youngest age group showed a 52% level in 'Not Good', whereas nearly half of the 15-39-year-olds, 49%, thought it was 'Very good'. Perhaps most amusingly, approximately half of the over-40s declined to comment in this area.

Overall, it is clear that the very young enjoyed books, the middle group enjoyed the Computer Software and DVDs (Non-Print) and the oldest either thought things were merely 'Satisfactory' or declined to comment.

***Word Count: 201***

所给的两份表格显示了有关居民对当地图书馆看法的调查结果。每份表格均按居民的年龄段划分，第一份表格显示了关于书籍范围的数据，第二份表格显示了"非印刷资料"。

更详细地看第一份表格中所示的"书籍范围"，可以很清楚地看到，不同年龄段的居民对什么是"非常好""令人满意"和"不好"有截然不同的观点。55%的15岁以下年龄段居民认为该书籍范围"非常好"，占比约为持有相同观点的其他两个年龄段居民（15～39岁和40岁以上）的两倍。认为该书籍范围"令人满意"的其他两个年龄段居民的百分比最高，分别为48%和50%。

继续看第二份表格中所示的"非印刷资料"，再次明显地看到被调查居民的意见有很大不同。最年轻的年龄段中有52%的居民认为非印刷资料"不好"，而15～39岁的年龄段中有近一半的居民（49%）认为非印刷资料"非常好"。也许最有趣的是，约一半40岁以上的居民拒绝在这方面发表评论。

总体而言，显然非常年轻的居民喜欢书，中间年龄段的居民喜欢电脑软件和数字影碟（非印刷），最年长的居民要么就相关事项的意见给出仅仅"令人满意"的选项，要么拒绝发表评论。

## Example 1　*Approach*

2G/T is the most logical here.

这种作文格式适合两张图表或表格的题型。

- Paragraph 1 – Table 1 – Compare age groups

  主体段 1——表格 1——比较年龄组

- Paragraph 2 – Table 2 – Compare age groups in the same order as P1

  主体段 2——表格 2——与主体段 1 的顺序一样比较年龄组

| Examiner's Comment | | | |
|---|---|---|---|
| Coherence and Cohesion | Logical | ☑ | |
| | Progression | Looking…first…, Moving on to, Overall | ☑ |
| Lexical Resource | Range | ☑ | |
| | Less Common | ☑ | |
| Grammatical Range and Accuracy | Simple Structures | ☑ | |
| | Complex Structures | ☑ | |

**Example 2** *Question and Answer*

*You should spend about 20 minutes on this task.*

> **The table below shows the number of cars made in three different countries from 2013 to 2019.**
>
> **Summarise the information by selecting and reporting the main features, and make comparisons where relevant.**

*Write at least 150 words.*

|           | 2013    | 2016      | 2019    |
|-----------|---------|-----------|---------|
| Argentina | 161,165 | 432, 121  | 512,935 |
| Australia | 413,251 | 330,960   | 227,253 |
| Malaysia  | 741,054 | 1,194,435 | 999,476 |

The table given depicts the differences between the number of cars made in 3 separate countries: Argentina, Australia and Malaysia, between 2013 and 2019.

Looking initially at Argentina's figures, we can see that from a beginning amount of a little more than 161,000, it more than tripled by the time when reaching 2019, with the final figure standing at 512,935.

Australia has the opposite trend. There, they started with slightly more than 410,000 and reduced their output by nearly half, ending up at 227,253.

Finally, viewing the Malaysian figures, these seemed to fluctuate. Firstly increasing from roughly 742,000 to nearly 1.2m, but then falling to rest at somewhat less than 1m. It is worth noting that the 2019 figure shows a 35% rise in output, though.

In summary, the only country that seemed to have stable growth was Argentina. The other two either declined or had a relatively unstable rise which is not particularly desirable.

***Word Count: 155***

所给表格描述了 2013 年至 2019 年阿根廷、澳大利亚和马来西亚这 3 个不同国家制造的汽车数量间的差异。

首先来看阿根廷制造的汽车数量。我们可以看到，该数量从最初的略多于 161,000 辆，到 2019 年时增加了两倍多，最终为 512,935 辆。

澳大利亚制造的汽车数量趋势与阿根廷相反。澳大利亚制造的汽车数量最初略多于 410,000 辆，之后汽车产量减少了近一半，最终汽车数量为 227,253 辆。

最后来看马来西亚制造的汽车数量，发现相关数字似乎有所波动。该数字首先从约 742,000 辆增加至近 1,200,000 辆，之后下降至略低于 1,000,000 辆。尽管如此，仍值得注意 2019 年的数据显示汽车产量增长了 35%。

总之，阿根廷似乎是唯一一个保持所制造汽车数量稳定增长的国家。澳大利亚和马来西亚制造汽车的数量要么下降，要么相对不稳定地上升，而这种情况不是特别理想。

## Example 2 *Approach*

3G/T is the most logical here.

这种作文格式适合三张图表或表格的题型。

- Paragraph 1 – Table data – Argentina

  主体段 1——表格数据——阿根廷

- Paragraph 2 – Table data – Australia

  主体段 2——表格数据——澳大利亚

- Paragraph 3 – Table data – Malaysia

  主体段 3——表格数据——马来西亚

| Examiner's Comment | | | |
|---|---|---|---|
| Coherence and Cohesion | Logical | ☑ | |
| | Progression | Looking initially, Finally, In summary | ☑ |
| Lexical Resource | Range | slightly more, increasing, rise; reduced, falling, declined | ☑ |
| | Less Common | depicts, roughly | ☑ |
| Grammatical Range and Accuracy | Simple Structures | ☑ | |
| | Complex Structures | ☑ | |

Example 3  *Question and Answer*

*You should spend about 20 minutes on this task.*

> The tables below show information about the temperature and hours of daylight in two different cities during a weekend in March 2017.
>
> Summarise the information by selecting and reporting the main features, and make comparisons where relevant.

*Write at least 150 words.*

| | New Dehli, India | | |
|---|---|---|---|
| | Friday | Saturday | Sunday |
| Temperature | Max: 33°C Min:29°C | Max: 34°C Min: 29°C | Max: 33°C Min: 29°C |
| Sunrise | 06.00 | 06.00 | 06.00 |
| Sunset | 19.11 | 19.11 | 19.13 |

| | Moscow, Russia | | |
|---|---|---|---|
| | Friday | Saturday | Sunday |
| Temperature | Max: 8°C Min: 5°C | Max: 13°C Min: 2°C | Max: 17°C Min: 9°C |
| Sunrise | 04.52 | 04.51 | 04.50 |
| Sunset | 22.02 | 22.04 | 22.06 |

The tables given illustrate the temperature and number of daylight hours in two different cities, New Dehli and Moscow, over the same weekend during the month of March in the year 2017.

Looking firstly at New Dehli, India, it is very noticeable that the data does not particularly change over the three days. Sunrise is at 6 a.m. on the dot, with sunset being 7.11 p.m. on the Friday and Saturday and two minutes later on the Sunday. With regards to the temperature, the minimum is 29 degrees Celsius across the time period, with the maximums being 33°C, 34°C and 33°C, respectively.

Moving onto the Moscow figures, these are all very different to New Dehli. Daylight gets progressively earlier: 4.52 a.m., 4.51 a.m., and then 4.50 a.m., with sunset gradually becoming later at 10.02 p.m., 10.04 p.m. and 10.06 p.m. The temperature is approximately 20 Degrees Celsius lower, with the data showing Friday's range as 5-8°C, Saturday's 2-13°C and Sunday's 9-17°C.

In summary, the data for the cities is quite different, with Moscow having longer daylight hours, but being much colder than New Dehli.

***Word Count: 184***

所给表格说明了2017年3月的同一个周末内新德里和莫斯科两个不同城市的温度和日照小时数。

首先看看印度新德里的情况。很明显，相关数据在3天内无特别变化。日出时间是早上6点整，星期五和星期六的日落时间是晚上7：11，星期天的日落时间晚两分钟。至于温度，这3天的最低温度均为29℃，最高温度分别为33℃、34℃和33℃。

继续看莫斯科的数据，这些数据均与新德里的相关数据截然不同。日出时间越来越早：分别为早上4：52、早上4：51和早上4：50，而日落时间越来越晚：分别为晚上10：02、晚上10：04和晚上10：06。气温大约低20℃，数据显示星期五的温度范围为5-8℃，星期六的温度范围为2-13℃，星期天的温度范围为9-17℃。

总之，新德里和莫斯科的数据差别很大，莫斯科的日照时数更长，但温度比新德里低得多。

## Example 3  *Approach*

2G/T is the most logical here.

这种作文格式适合两张图表或表格的题型。

- Paragraph 1 – Table 1 data – New Dehli, India

  主体段1——表格1数据——印度新德里

- Paragraph 2 – Table 2 data – Moscow, Russia – Compare to New Dehli, India

  主体段2——表格2数据——俄罗斯莫斯科——与印度新德里比较

| Examiner's Comment | | | |
|---|---|---|---|
| Coherence and Cohesion | Logical | ☑ | |
| | Progression | Looking firstly, Moving onto, In summary | ☑ |
| Lexical Resource | Range | ☑ | |
| | Less Common | illustrate, approximately | ☑ |
| Grammatical Range and Accuracy | Simple Structures | ☑ | |
| | Complex Structures | ☑ | |

Example 4    *Question and Answer*

*You should spend about 20 minutes on this task.*

> **The table below shows information about high school teachers' salaries in five different countries in 2019.**
>
> **Summarise the information by selecting and reporting the main features, and make comparisons where relevant.**

*Write at least 150 words.*

| Country | Annual Salary (US$) | | | Years taken to reach top salary |
|---------|----------|---------------|---------|------------------|
| | Starting | After 15 years | Maximum | |
| Australia | 34,600 | 48,000 | 48,000 | 9 |
| Holland | 47,000 | 54,000 | 54,000 | 8 |
| Japan | 28,000 | 49,000 | 62,400 | 30 |
| Korea | 30,500 | 52,600 | 84,500 | 37 |
| Luxembourg | 70,000 | 112,000 | 139,000 | 34 |

**High School teachers' salaries in 2019**

The table given illustrates information about teachers' incomes, in USD, in five different countries in 2019 – Starting, After 15 years and Maximum. The countries are, from top to bottom, Australia, Holland, Japan, Korea, and Luxembourg.

Looking first at the lowest and highest starting points, it can be clearly seen that Japan has the lowest initial salary, with $28,000 rising to $49,000 after 15 years and a maximum of $62,400 after 30 years. Luxembourg starts at more than double that of Japan, at $70,000, increasing by $42,000 at the 15-year mark and reaching $139,000 after 34 years.

The other three countries are fairly similar, with Korean, Australian and Holland's beginning salaries being $30,500, $34,600 and $47,000, respectively. They all go up similarly, reaching the maximum in 15 years, except Korea, listing $30,500, $52,600 and $84,500.

In summary, it seems the best place to be a teacher from start to finish is Luxembourg.

**Word Count: 152**

所给表格显示了2019年5个不同国家的教师收入信息（以美元计）——起始薪资、15年后薪资和最高薪资。这些国家从上到下依次是澳大利亚、荷兰、日本、韩国和卢森堡。

　　首先看看教师收入的最低和最高起点，可以清楚地看到日本教师的起薪最低，15年后从28,000美元涨至49,000美元，30年后最高为62,400美元。卢森堡教师的起薪是日本教师的2倍多，为70,000美元，15年后增加了42,000美元，34年后达到139,000美元。

　　其他3个国家的教师收入情况十分类似，韩国教师、澳大利亚教师和荷兰教师的起薪分别为30,500美元、34,600美元和47,000美元。这3个国家教师的起薪上涨情况差不多，15年后澳大利亚教师、荷兰教师的薪资达到最高，除韩国外，其薪资分别为30,500美元、52,600美元和84,500美元。

　　总之，似乎自始至终教师收入最高的国家是卢森堡。

## Example 4　*Approach*

1G/T is the most logical here.

这种作文格式适合一张图表或表格的题型。

- Paragraph 1 – Table data – Lowest and Highest Salary

  主体段1——表格数据——最低薪资和最高薪资

- Paragraph 2 – Table data – Other data – Compare within data

  主体段2——表格数据——其他数据——数据之间进行比较

| Examiner's Comment | | | |
|---|---|---|---|
| Coherence and Cohesion | Logical | ☑ | |
| | Progression | Looking first, The other three, In summary | ☑ |
| Lexical Resource | Range | rising, increasing, go up | ☑ |
| | Less Common | illustrates, initial | ☑ |
| Grammatical Range and Accuracy | Simple Structures | ☑ | |
| | Complex Structures | ☑ | |

Example 5   *Question and Answer*

*You should spend about 20 minutes on this task.*

> **The table below shows information about salaries for different age groups and if they have graduated, or not, from university.**
>
> **Summarise the information by selecting and reporting the main features, and make comparisons where relevant.**

*Write at least 150 words.*

### Average Salaries (all age groups) in the UK

|  | Graduates | Non-Graduates |
|---|---|---|
| Average Salary | £35,100 | £17,460 |

### Average Salaries (different age groups) in the UK

| Age | Graduates | Non-Graduates |
|---|---|---|
| 22 | £17,800 | £14,500 |
| 35 | £31,800 | £19,100 |
| 45 | £32,800 | £19,100 |
| 55 | £53,100 | £18,200 |
| 60 | £55,100 | £15,300 |

The tables given show information about UK salaries for those that have completed university and those that have not between the ages of 22 and 60 as well as the overall average.

Firstly, looking at the average, it is shown that the graduate's salary is £35,100, whereas, for non-graduates, it is only £17,460.

Moving on to the breakdown by age, graduates begin at £17,800 and then jump to £31,800 by 35. This gradually increases over the next 25 years to reach a peak of £55,100 when nearing retirement age, at 60.

For the non-graduates, the starting amount is fairly similar at £14,500 but peaks at £19,100 and stays there for the next 20 years. At 55, this reduces slightly to £18,200 and then again falls a little more drastically to £15,300 for those after 60.

In summary, it is clear that graduates earn far more than those who have not been to university.

**Word Count: 153**

所给表格显示了年龄在22岁至60岁之间的英国大学毕业生和非大学毕业生的薪资信息以及各自的总体薪资平均值。

首先看看大学毕业生和非大学毕业生的总体薪资平均值，表格显示大学毕业生的薪资是35,100英镑，而非大学毕业生的薪资只有17,460英镑。

接着从年龄分类看，发现大学毕业生的起薪为17,800英镑，到35岁时猛增至31,800英镑。在接下来的25年里，该数字逐渐上升，在接近退休年龄（60岁）时最高达到55,100英镑。

非大学毕业生的起薪与大学毕业生的起薪情况十分相似，为14,500英镑，最高为19,100英镑，并在接下来的20年里保持不变。55岁时，该数字略微下降至18,200英镑，60岁后，该数字又大幅下降至15,300英镑。

总之，显然大学毕业生的收入远远高于非大学毕业生的收入。

## Example 5　*Approach*

2G/T is the most logical here.

这种作文结构适合两张图表或表格的题型。

- Paragraph 1 – Table 1 data – Average Salary

  主体段1——表格1数据——平均薪资

- Paragraph 2 – Table 2 data – Graduates

  主体段2——表格2数据——大学毕业生

- Paragraph 3 – Table 2 data – Non-Graduates

  主体段3——表格2数据——非大学毕业生

| Examiner's Comment | | | |
|---|---|---|---|
| Coherence and Cohesion | Logical | ☑ | |
| | Progression | Firstly, Moving on to, In summary | ☑ |
| Lexical Resource | Range | jump, increases; reduces, falls | ☑ |
| | Less Common | peaks, drastically | ☑ |
| Grammatical Range and Accuracy | Simple Structures | ☑ | |
| | Complex Structures | ☑ | |

Example 6  *Question and Answer*

*You should spend about 20 minutes on this task.*

> **The table below shows the percentage of residents in four kinds of living places in different regions in a particular city in the UK in 2020.**
>
> **Summarise the information by selecting and reporting the main features, and make comparisons where relevant.**

*Write at least 150 words.*

| Areas<br>Types of Housing | Central Area<br>(pop: 31,700) | North Area<br>(pop: 32,100) | South Area<br>(pop: 32,000) |
|---|---|---|---|
| Detached House | 15% | 38% | 12% |
| Semi-Detached House | 34% | 37% | 14% |
| Terraced House | 13% | 15% | 39% |
| Flat and Apartment | 38% | 10% | 35% |

The table depicts four different types of accommodation in the UK in 2020. The kinds listed are Detached, Semi-Detached, Terraced Houses and also Flats/Apartments. The data is also divided into areas of the city, Central, North and South.

Starting with the Central area, it seems, perhaps unsurprisingly, that Flats/Apartments are the most popular with 38%, closely followed by semi-detached houses with 34%. Detached and then Terraced housing comprise the remaining 28%, with 15% and 13%, respectively.

Moving north now, the figures are quite different. Detached and Semi-Detached are the favourites in this area, with 38% and 37%. Terraced Houses and Flats make up the remaining 25%.

Finally, in the southern area, the figures are quite different again, with Terraced Housing and Flats at the top showing 39% and 35%. Detached and Semi-Detached have a near-even split on the remaining 26%, with semis having slightly more.

In summary, it appears that each area has two distinct types of preferred housing that are mostly different from each of the other regions.

***Word Count: 169***

该表格描述了2020年英国的4种不同住处类型的情况。表格中列出的住处类型有独立式房屋、半独立式房屋、连栋房屋和公寓。表格中也按照划分的城市各区域（即中心区域、北部区域和南部区域）列出数据。

首先看中心区域，发现公寓似乎最受欢迎，占比为38%，紧随其后的是半独立式房屋，占比为34%，这或许并不令人意外。剩余28%是由独立式房屋和连栋房屋构成，分别占15%和13%。

现在继续看北部区域，发现相关数据与中心区域的数据大不相同。在北部区域，独立式房屋和半独立式房屋最受欢迎，分别占38%和37%。剩余25%是连栋房屋和公寓。

最后，在南部区域，相关数字也与中心区域和北部区域的数字大不相同，连栋房屋和公寓最受欢迎，分别占39%和35%。剩余26%为独立式房屋和半独立式房屋，二者的占比几乎相同，但半独立式房屋的占比略高。

总之，似乎每个区域均有两种截然不同的首选住房类型，且都与其他区域的情况大不相同。

## Example 6    *Approach*

1G/T is the most logical here.

这种作文格式适合一张图表或表格的题型。

- Paragraph 1 – Table data – Central

  主体段1——表格数据——中心区域

- Paragraph 2 – Table data – North

  主体段2——表格数据——北部区域

- Paragraph 3 – Table data – South

  主体段3——表格数据——南部区域

*This could also have been divided by type of house, but I thought it would be more understandable to the reader if the figures added up to 100% (as they do in the columns, but not the rows).*

也可以根据房屋类型来分段，但我认为对于读者来说，如果数据加在一起是100%会更容易理解（如这里的纵栏数据，不是横栏数据）。

| Examiner's Comment | | | |
|---|---|---|---|
| Coherence and Cohesion | Logical | ☑ | |
| | Progression | Starting, Moving...now, Finally, In summary | ☑ |
| Lexical Resource | Range | divided, split | ☑ |
| | Less Common | depicts, distinct, preferred | ☑ |
| Grammatical Range and Accuracy | Simple Structures | ☑ | |
| | Complex Structures | ☑ | |

## ■ Maps

Example 1   *Question and Answer*

*You should spend about 20 minutes on this task.*

> **The plans below show a small park in 1980 and the park in the present.**
>
> **Summarise the information by selecting and reporting the main features, and make comparisons where relevant.**

*Write at least 150 words.*

**Map of a Park**

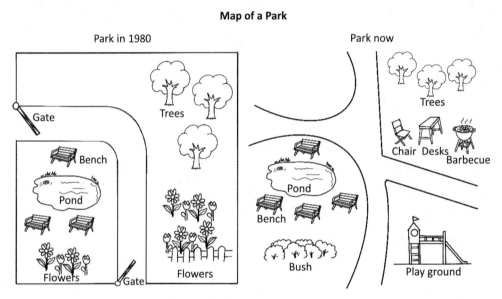

There are two pictures shown. The first shows the park as it was in 1980, and the second depicts it now.

Firstly, looking at the park as it was 40-odd years ago, we can see that there was a single path going from the south gate and ending in the northwest corner. There were two flower beds, one on each side, at the entrance, with some trees in the east and northeast, whereas there was a pond north of the western flower bed.

Moving onto the park as it is now, the only thing that seems to have remained the same is the pond's location. Some bushes have replaced the southwestern flower bed, and the south-eastern one is now a sports area. Picnic tables and a barbeque area are now amongst the north-eastern trees. Lastly, the gates have been removed, and pathways cross the entire park.

In summary, there seem to have been considerable changes to almost all areas of the park.

***Word Count: 162***

本题显示了两张图片。第一张图片显示了该公园在1980年的状况，第二张图片则显示了该公园的现状。

首先看40多年前的公园，我们可以看到有一条从公园南门到公园西北角的小路。公园入口处有两个花坛，一边一个，东侧和东北侧种有一些树，西侧花坛的北面有一个池塘。

继续看公园现状，发现唯一保持不变的似乎是池塘的位置。部分灌木已取代公园西南侧的花坛，公园东南侧的花坛现在变成运动区。野餐桌和烧烤区现在位于公园东北侧的树木之间。最后，公园大门已拆除，同时多条道路穿过整个公园。

总之，公园几乎所有区域似乎都发生了相当大的变化。

## Example 1  *Approach*

2M is the most logical here.

这种作文格式适合两张地图的题型。

- Paragraph 1 – Park Data 1980

  主体段 1——1980年的公园布局

- Paragraph 2 – Park Data now – Compare to P1

  主体段 2——当前的公园布局——与主体段 1 比较

| Examiner's Comment | | | |
|---|---|---|---|
| Coherence and Cohesion | Logical | √ | |
| | Progression | Firstly, Moving onto, Lastly, In summary | √ |
| Lexical Resource | Range | √ | |
| | Less Common | depicts, amongst, considerable | √ |
| Grammatical Range and Accuracy | Simple Structures | √ | |
| | Complex Structures | √ | |

Example 2   *Question and Answer*

*You should spend about 20 minutes on this task.*

> **The plans below show a Biology School at a university now and in the future.**
>
> **Summarise the information by selecting and reporting the main features, and make comparisons where relevant.**

*Write at least 150 words.*

**The future plan about the Biology School in a particular university**

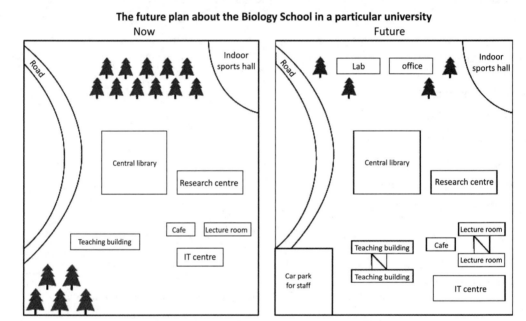

The maps provided illustrate the Biology School in an unnamed university. The left-hand picture shows it as it is currently, with the right-hand side showing a future development plan.

To begin with, in the current layout, we can see that the whole area is surrounded by woodland on the northern and southwestern sides, with an access road on the western side. The central library is centrally located, with a research centre on its eastern side. To the south of these buildings are a teaching building on the southwest side, a café, a lecture room, and an IT centre on the southeast side. The last area in the very northeast is where an indoor sports hall has been built.

Looking at the future map, several significant changes are being planned. Perhaps the largest of these is the addition of a lab and an office replacing much of the woodland in the north and a staff car park replacing the trees in the southwest. An additional teaching building and lecture room are being added and connected to the existing buildings.

Overall, much of the expansion is to the north and southwest at the expense of the surrounding woodland.

***Word Count: 196***

所提供的地图说明了某所大学的生物学院情况。左图显示了该生物学院现状，右图则显示了该生物学院的未来开发平面图。

首先，在当前布局中，我们可以看到整个区域由北侧和西南侧的林地包围，在西侧有一条通道。中央图书馆位于中心位置，其东侧设有一个研究中心。在这些建筑南面，西南侧有一栋教学楼，东南侧有一家咖啡馆、一间教室和一个信息技术中心。东北角的最后一个区域建有一个室内体育馆。

继续看未来地图，发现有若干项重大变化正在规划中。其中最大的变化可能是增建实验室和办公室，取代生物学院北侧的大部分林地，并增建教职工停车场，取代生物学院西南侧的树木。正在增建另外的教学楼和教室，并与现有建筑相连。

总体而言，大部分扩建均以生物学院周围林地为代价向生物学院的北侧和西南侧进行。

## Example 2  *Approach*

2M is the most logical here.

这种作文格式适合两张地图的题型。

● Paragraph 1 – Biology School Data Now

   主体段 1——生物学院当前布局

● Paragraph 2 – Biology School Data Future – Compare to P1

   主体段 2——生物学院未来开发平面图——与主体段 1 比较

*Tiny Tip:* *Even though the map doesn't show a compass, assuming up is north is standard practice.*

**小提示：**尽管地图上没有指南针，但假设上方是北方是标准做法。

| Examiner's Comment | | | |
| --- | --- | --- | --- |
| Coherence and Cohesion | Logical | | ☑ |
| | Progression | To begin with, Looking at, Overall | ☑ |
| Lexical Resource | Range | centre, building | ☑ |
| | Less Common | illustrate, significant, expansion, expense of | ☑ |
| Grammatical Range and Accuracy | Simple Structures | ☑ | |
| | Complex Structures | ☑ | |

# ■ Process

Example 1 *Question and Answer*

*You should spend about 20 minutes on this task.*

> **The process below shows one of the ways to manufacture ceramic pots.**
>
> **Summarise the information by selecting and reporting the main features, and make comparisons where relevant.**

*Write at least 150 words.*

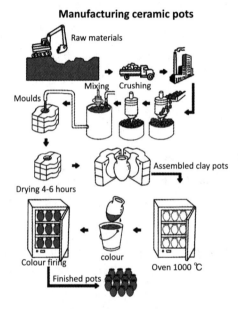

**Manufacturing ceramic pots**

The given diagram depicts a process used in order to make a ceramic pot. It is noted as 'one way' to make them rather than 'the' way, which insinuates that there are multiple procedures that can be followed.

It all starts with the clay, or 'raw materials', being extracted from the ground using machinery similar to JCB's. This is then transported, using trucks, to a factory. The unprocessed clay is placed on a conveyor belt at the factory and transported to be crushed. After initial crushing, the clay is then further crushed, presumably into a fine powder, and then mixed with water and piped into pre-fabricated moulds.

After 4-6 hours of drying, the 'assembled' clay pot is placed in an oven, or kiln, for an unspecified amount of time at 1000 degrees centigrade. Colour is then added to each pot, and they are placed in another oven for the colour to be 'fired'.

After all this has been completed, the pots are ready to be packed, shipped and sold.

***Word Count: 169***

所给图表描述了制作陶瓷罐的过程。该过程被称为"一种方式"而不是"特定"方式，这暗示着有多种程序可遵循。

制作陶瓷罐的过程都从黏土即"原材料"开始，使用类似于JCB品牌的机器从地下提取黏土。之后用卡车将黏土运输至工厂。将未加工的黏土置于工厂的传送带上，之后运送其进行粉碎。完成初步粉碎后，进一步粉碎黏土，大概会变成细粉，之后加水与之混合，接着用管道将混合物输送到预制模具中。

干燥4-6小时后，将"组装完成的"陶罐置于烤炉或窑炉中，在1000 ℃下烧制一段时间。接着给每个陶罐上色，之后将陶罐置于另一个烤炉里"烧制"颜色。

完成所有这些步骤后，陶罐就可以包装、运输和出售了。

---

**Example 1**  *Approach*

1P is the most logical here.

这种作文格式适合一张流程图的题型。

● Paragraph 1 – Raw Materials → Moulds

主体段1——原材料 → 模具

● Paragraph 2 – Drying → Finished Pots

主体段2——干燥 → 制作好的陶罐

| Examiner's Comment | | | |
|---|---|---|---|
| Coherence and Cohesion | Logical | ☑ | |
| | Progression | It all starts, This is then, is then added, After all | ☑ |
| Lexical Resource | Range | transported, assembled | ☑ |
| | Less Common | extracted, unprocessed, kiln | ☑ |
| Grammatical Range and Accuracy | Simple Structures | ☑ | |
| | Complex Structures | ☑ | |

Example 2    *Question and Answer*

*You should spend about 20 minutes on this task.*

> **The process chart below shows the typical process someone must go through when applying for a driving licence in the US.**
>
> **Summarise the information by selecting and reporting the main features, and make comparisons where relevant.**

*Write at least 150 words.*

**Driving Licence Application Process**

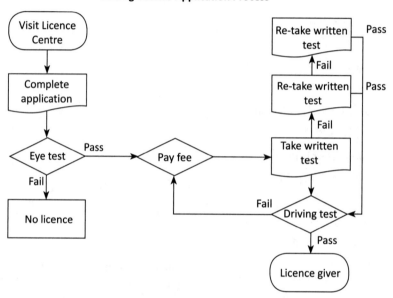

The flow chart process given illustrates how people in the US can obtain a driving licence. It seems to be broken down into three main stages: at the licence centre, payment, and testing.

When looking at the first part, prospective drivers must initially visit the licence centre and complete an application form. Once this is achieved, an eye test is performed. If this is failed, people will not be able to apply further. If passed, they will need to pay a fee. The amount of the fee is not shown.

Moving onto the testing section, two different tests are shown: a written test and a driving test. The written test comes first, and candidates are given three attempts to pass this. They must pay the fee again if they fail after the third attempt. If they pass, they will move on to the practical driving test. Only one attempt is allowed at this. If they fail, people must make an additional payment. However, if they pass it, they will receive a valid US driving licence.

***Word Count: 174***

所给的流程图过程说明了美国的人们获得驾驶执照的方式。该过程似乎分为3个主要阶段：在驾驶执照中心、付款和测试。

看第一个阶段时，准驾驶员必须首先前往驾驶执照中心填写一份申请表。填写完申请表后，需要进行视力测试。如果视力测试不合格，准驾驶员将无法进一步申请获得驾驶执照。如果视力测试合格，准驾驶员将需要支付一笔费用。该费用金额并未显示。

继续看测试阶段，图中显示了两种不同的测试：笔试和驾驶考试。首先是笔试，考生有3次机会通过笔试。如果使用第三次机会后仍然未通过笔试，考生必须再次付费。如果通过笔试，考生将继续参加实操驾驶考试。该考试只允许考生有一次机会。如果未能通过实操驾驶考试，考生必须再次付费。但是，如果考生通过实操驾驶考试，他们将获得有效的美国驾驶执照。

---

**Example 2** *Approach*

**1P is the most logical here.**

这种作文格式适合一张流程图的题型。

● Paragraph 1 – Application and Fee

   主体段 1——申请和费用

● Paragraph 2 – Different Tests

   主体段 2——不同的测试

| Examiner's Comment | | | |
|---|---|---|---|
| Coherence and Cohesion | Logical | ☑ | |
| | Progression | ...the first part, Moving onto | ☑ |
| Lexical Resource | Range | people, prospective drivers, candidates | ☑ |
| | Less Common | achieved, additional | ☑ |
| Grammatical Range and Accuracy | Simple Structures | ☑ | |
| | Complex Structures | ☑ | |

**Example 1**   *Question and Answer*

*You should spend about 20 minutes on this task.*

You have just received a credit card statement from your bank. The statement lists a number of expensive purchases that you are sure you did not make.

Write a letter to the bank manager. In the letter:

- Introduce yourself.
- Explain that you did not buy the items listed.
- Say what you would like the bank to do to fix the problem.

***You do not need to write any addresses. Begin your letter as follows:***

Dear Sir or Madam,

***You should write at least 150 words.***

Dear Sir or Madam,

My name is James Foster, and my credit card number is 12345. I am writing to query some expensive items that have appeared on my most recent credit card statement.

The items were a Louis Vuitton bag purchased on the 13th, a watch purchased in Harrod's on the same day and a PS5 console bought from Game on the 14th. You will notice from your records that I called to report that my credit card had been stolen on the 12th of last month. I spoke with John and was given the reference number ABCD1.

I am very concerned that these items are still appearing on my statement with a payment expected to cover their cost. I would be very grateful if you could look into the matter, have these items, and any others that may appear after the 12th, removed and a new statement sent out to me.

If you have any queries, you can contact me by phone on 0765432109 or via email at james@foster.com.

I look forward to hearing from you.

Yours faithfully,

James Foster

***Word Count: 182***

尊敬的先生或女士：

我叫詹姆斯·福斯特（James Foster），我的信用卡号是12345。我写这封信是想要询问有关一些出现在我最近的信用卡账单上的昂贵物品的情况。

这些物品包括13日购买的一个路易威登包、同一天在哈罗德百货公司购买的一块手表和14日从Game公司购买的一台PS5游戏机。经查看你们的记录，你会发现，我在上个月12日致电报告过我的信用卡被盗的事件。我曾与约翰（John）交谈，并获得了参考号ABCD 1。

我非常担心我的账单继续出现这些物品，并预期付款来支付这些物品的费用。如果你能调查此事，将这些物品以及12日以后可能出现的任何其他物品从我的信用卡账单中删除，并给我发送一份新的信用卡账单，我将不胜感激。

如果有任何疑问，可通过致电0765432109或发送电子邮件至james@foster.com与我联系。

期待你的回信。

此致

詹姆斯·福斯特

---

Example 1　*Approach*

1Gen would be the correct approach here.

这种作文格式适合一般的培训类书信题型。

- P1 – Introduce myself – Give my name and credit card number

  主体段1——介绍自己——给出名字与信用卡号

- P2 – Mention items and my card was stolen, therefore I didn't buy them

  主体段2——提及刷卡记录以及信用卡被盗事实，所以我并没有买以上东西

- P3 – What I want them to do – Take the items off and send a new statement

  主体段3——我希望他们怎样处理——将这些消费记录销掉并发给我一张新的账单

- Close off letter.

  结束此信。

| | | Examiner's Comment | |
|---|---|---|---|
| Coherence and Cohesion | Logical | ☑ | |
| | Progression | My name is, The items were, ... look into the matter..., any queries | ☑ |
| Lexical Resource | Range | purchased, bought | ☑ |
| | Less Common | stolen, reference, appearing, grateful | ☑ |
| Grammatical Range and Accuracy | Simple Structures | ☑ | |
| | Complex Structures | ☑ | |

Congratulations on finishing this part of the book! After going through these examples, I hope you better understand how to approach and structure your Task 1 essays.

恭喜你读完了本书这一部分！看完这些例文后，我希望你能更好地理解如何处理和组织你的 Task 1 文章。

Please don't just memorise these answers. You will need to analyse how I sorted the data and then described it. Once you have understood the concepts, it won't matter what the question is because you'll be able to process the data on your own, choose the appropriate approach and then confidently write your essays.

不要只是死记硬背这些答案。你需要分析我是如何对数据进行分类和描述的。一旦你理解了这些概念，不论遇到什么问题都可以处理，因为你已经可以自己分析处理数据，选择合适的方法，然后自信地写出自己的作文。

As I mentioned earlier, I suggest you write Task 1 after Task 2. This is mainly because Task 1 is worth fewer points toward your overall writing score than Task 2, but it's also because once you've had a lot of practice at Task 1, it becomes very easy and quick to complete. It's perfectly possible to complete this task in 15 minutes or maybe even less.

正如我之前提到的，我建议你在写完 Task 2 之后再写 Task 1。主要因为 Task 1 的分值占总分的比例要低于 Task 2。但也因为一旦你在 Task 1 上进行了大量的练习，它就会变得非常容易和快速完成。在 15 分钟甚至更短的时间内完成是很有可能的。

# Section III

# Task 2 Preparation and Question Types

# Task 2 备考及问题类型

In this section, I will provide examples of Task 2 question types that **may** appear in the IELTS Writing exam. Please DO NOT just blindly memorise these answers. Look at them, learn any unfamiliar words and how to use them, and understand why I'm using those words or the grammar structures to create your answers for the exam.

在这一部分，我将提供一些**可能**出现在雅思写作考试 Task 2 中的题目及例文。但请不要只是盲目地背诵这些答案。仔细阅读，学习任何不熟悉的单词及如何使用它们，并理解为什么我会使用这些单词或语法结构，进而写出自己的作文。

*Disclaimer: The answers I've written are provided as examples of the different scores based on the information given in the Public IELTS Writing criteria. They do not guarantee that anyone would achieve those scores in a real IELTS exam and should be taken as guidelines only. It should also be understood that the marks given by examiners are for the task as a whole, not the individual paragraphs or sentences.*

**免责声明：** 本书中不同分数的答案范例的依据标准是公众版雅思写作评分标准。这些答案不能保证任何人在实际的雅思考试中取得相应的分数，在此仅供参考。同时需要清楚，考官在写作考试中是给文章整体打分，而不是给每个部分单独打分。

It should be understood that the example answers don't necessarily represent my actual beliefs. They are simply what came to my mind at the time of writing. Don't forget, the examiner is not marking you on your opinion. They are marking you on your ability to express that opinion in written form. 99.9% of the time, the examiner doesn't care what you think of a situation. The only time this may change is if you write something that's particularly offensive or dangerous to a group of people.

有一点需要理解，例文并不代表我自己的实际观点。它们只是我写作时的想法。别忘了，考官不是根据你的观点来打分。他们是就你是否有能力以书面形式表达观点来打分。**99.9%** 的情况下，考官并不关心你所持的立场。唯一需要做改变的情况是，如果你写的内容会冒犯某些人或让他们觉得危险。

# Chapter 1 Task 2 Preparation
## Task 2 备考

As mentioned previously, Task 2 mostly concerns whether you can produce a structured essay about a given topic. Similarly to Task 1, all essays should be structured with a Beginning, Middle and End.

如前所述，**Task 2** 主要考查你是否可以根据题目要求写出结构清晰的作文。与 **Task 1** 相似，所有的作文结构都包括开头段、中间主体段及结尾段。

The beginning or 'Introduction' should rephrase/reword the main statement and should inform the reader of the plan of the essay. The Middle or 'Body' of the text should be split into 2, or very occasionally 3, paragraphs and will be the main substance of your ideas/opinions about the topic given in the Task. The End or 'Conclusion' should definitely provide the reader with your opinion or overall thoughts.

开头段应该重新表述题目中的内容，并告知读者文章的计划。主体段落应该分成 2 段，偶尔也可以分成 3 段，是对话题内容或观点的主要论述。结尾段可以再次向读者说明你的观点或总体想法。

When approaching Task 2, the first thing that you need to make sure of is that you properly understand the style of essay that is required. These are covered in detail over the following few pages and will help you understand the necessary structures and thinking processes. Once this has been achieved, the second step is to analyse the question to understand it correctly. This can be done by identifying the keywords of the task statement as exampled below:

当看到 **Task 2** 的题目时，你需要确保的第一件事是清楚题目要求的写作类型。这些细节将在接下来的几页中详细介绍，并帮助你更加了解 **Task 2** 的结构与思考步骤。当这一步完成后，第二步就是分析题目并正确理解其内容。这可以通过找出题目中的关键词来完成，如下例：

***Employers should give their staff at least four weeks' holiday a year to make employees better at their work.***

In the example above, the keywords/phrases can be listed as:

在上面的例子中，关键词或短语可以如下：

***Employers, give staff, 4 weeks holiday, year, employees better at work***

From these words/phrases, we can tell who is being talked about and what. The other words aren't always needed as they add no more meaning to what we already have. It's important, however, sometimes, that these 'ignored' words are understood in case they have any subtle meaning. It should also be understood that they occasionally use synonyms, like in the example above – staff, and employees.

从这些单词或短语中，我们可以知道围绕谁在谈论，以及谈论的内容。其他的词并不总是必要的，因为不会在我们已知信息的基础上增加更多的意义。然而，有时候理解这些"被忽略"的词是很重要的，以防它们有任何微妙的含义。还应该理解的是，题目里偶尔会使用同义词，如同上例——staff 和 employees。

As you'll find out later in this book, you can potentially lose several marks if your answer is 'tangential', which means that your answer is not entirely related to the question. The primary reason that this happens is that the question hasn't been FULLY understood.

正如在本书后面的介绍中你会发现，如果你的答案是"离题的"，这意味着你的答案与问题不完全相关，你可能会被扣分。发生这种情况的主要原因是你没有完全理解这个题目。

*Important Tip:* *I would suggest 50-60 words for both the Introduction and Conclusion (100-120 in total), and then 70-90 words in each of the two paragraphs (140-180 in total). This looks more pleasing to the eye, as it is quite balanced and gives you a target to achieve for each section that, with practice, is reasonably easy to reach and means that you don't need to check your Word Count unless absolutely necessary.*

**重要提示：**我建议开头段与结尾段各写 50-60 字（共计 100-120 字），主体段两段每段各写 70-90 字（共计 140-180 字）。这种布局不仅看起来比较舒服，也比较平衡，使你在行文中会更加清晰每段要达成的目标，经过一段时间的练习后，你会发现除非特别必要，否则不需要检查字数就可以轻松完成。

*Tiny Tip:* *In each of the tasks, the examiner is expecting a total of four paragraphs. If you write a different number of paragraphs, make sure that you know why!*

**小提示：**在每篇作文中，考官会期待看到四个段落。如果你写的段落数量不同，请确保你知道为什么这样写！

# Question Types and Different Approaches

In 'The Examination Structure', I briefly mentioned the varying types of questions that often appear in the exam and will now discuss them in more detail.

在前面的"写作考试结构"这部分中，我简要地提到了考试中经常出现的不同类型的问题，在这一部分我会更详细地来讨论。

▶ **Discuss both these views and give your own opinion.** 讨论这两种观点并给出你自己的观点。

This phrase indicates that the answer needs to have a balanced argument and that you need to understand it from both sides and then tell the reader which side you're on.

这句话表明在作答时需要有一个平衡的论点，你需要对两种观点都理解并且告诉读者你支持哪个观点。

Perhaps one of the most common issues/mistakes that happen in this type of essay is at the end. Namely, that the candidate doesn't choose a side. It's important to understand that the examiner doesn't mind which side of the argument you're on, just that you can tell them that you're on a side. Suggesting that there are arguments on both sides is a weak position, not to mention an overly obvious statement when referring to this kind of question. So, it's crucial that you PICK A SIDE when writing this essay and then use the appropriate phrases throughout your essay to show that (refer to Task Response level 7).

考生在写这类作文时最常在文末出错。也就是说，考生没有选择自己的立场。明白这一点很重要，考官并不介意你支持的是哪一种观点，只要你能说明你的观点。两种立场都面面俱到的论证会使文章观点不明显，更不用说在面对这类题型时更需要提出鲜明的观点。所以，在写这类作文时，选择你所支持的观点，并且在整篇文章中使用适当的短语来表明这一点是至关重要的（在7分作文任务回应标准中有提及）。

An example from one of the main body paragraphs could begin:

主体段落第一句可以如下例这样写：

*There are those, of which I'm not one, that believe ...*

The overall structure of the essay should look like the following:

文章的整体结构应该如下所示：

| Introduction<br>开头段 | Rewriting the initial statement and indicating the plan of your essay.<br>重申题目，并表明你的文章内容计划。 |
| --- | --- |

| Main Body Paragraph 1<br>主体段第1段 | 1st side of the argument including a statement, reason and an example.<br>论证一种观点，列出原因并举出一个例证。 |
|---|---|
| Main Body Paragraph 2<br>主体段第2段 | 2nd side of the argument including a statement, reason and an example.<br>论证另一种观点，列出原因并举出一个例证。 |
| Conclusion<br>结尾段 | Which side you believe to be correct and why.<br>表明你支持哪一种观点并阐明原因。 |

▶ **To what extent do you agree or disagree? 你在多大程度上同意或不同意？**

This phrasing can sometimes be a little confusing. Firstly, let me say that has very little to do with 'Discuss both these views …'. Here are a couple of the reasons why:

这个措词会让人有点困惑。首先，我要说的是，这与 Discuss both these views … 完全不同。这里有几个原因：

1. This type is a question, 'Discuss both these views …', is not. This means that you have a choice in your answer. 这类题目是一个问题，而 Discuss both these views … 并不是。这表明你在作答这类时可以有自己的选择。

2. You don't need to write both sides of this argument. In the 'Discuss both views …', you do. 在这类题目中，你不需要两种观点都写。而在 Discuss both views … 的题目中，你需要两种观点都提到。

To me, the most critical element of this question is the first part; 'To what extent …?'. Another way of phrasing this would be 'How much?'. For the higher marks in Writing Task 2, it's insufficient to simply write 'I agree' or 'I disagree' as it doesn't completely answer the question and will lead to a reduced 'Task Response' score. It would be best to let the examiner know that you 'completely' or 'totally' agree or disagree. Partially agreeing, again, as described above, is too much in the middle of the argument and, structurally, is much harder to write.

对于我来说，这个题目最关键的部分是一开始问到 To what extent …? 换种说法就是 How much …? 在 Task 2 中如果要获得高分，只是表明"我同意"或"我不同意"是不够的，因为它并没有充分回答问题，因此在"任务回应"的评判标准下会失分。最好是让考官知道你"完全"或"非常"同意或不同意。如果只是像刚刚提到的部分同意，夹在两种观点之间，从结构上来讲，也比较难写。

In order to receive at least a partial tick for Task Response Level 7 (presents a clear position throughout the response) make sure that you open each paragraph with a phrase like:

为了在任务回应的7分评分标准中至少达成一项（回应写作任务过程中始终呈现一个清晰的观点），请确保你在每个段落的开头都用这样的短语：

● I believe that …

● Others, of which I'm one, believe that …

● In my opinion …

Make sure that the first sentence of each paragraph indicates the subject of the paragraph. The second sentence will generally be the reason why you think in the way that you stated in your topic sentence (paragraph sentence 1). From there, I'd advise you to give an example from '…your own knowledge or experience.'. You need to repeat this structure for the second paragraph.

确保每段的第一句话表明该段的主题。第二句通常是你在主题句（段落第一句）里所提出观点的原因。之后，我建议你以 … your own knowledge or experience 句式举出一个例子。你需要在主体段第 2 段重复这种结构。

Your summary should be whatever you put in the 2 paragraph body, in brief. For this type of question, I suggest that you use phrases like:

在总结段中，简单重申你在主体段落中的观点。这种题型的常用短语如下：

• In summary,

• To sum up,

• In short, etc.

Rather than something like – 'In conclusion,'. For me, a Summary and a Conclusion are not the same and are used for different purposes. Put simply, a Summary is your content rewritten in a brief way; a Conclusion is written after making some kind of decision or assessing some results. So, you could use a conclusion in a 'Discuss both these views and give your own opinion.' essay, but you can't for this type (To what extent do you agree or disagree?).

而不是用 In conclusion。对我而言，因为 Summary 和 Conclusion 的意义不同，两个词语的使用目的也不同。简单来说，Summary 就是换一种说法简短重申你已表述的内容，即摘要；而 Conclusion 是在做出某种决定或评估某些结果后的结论。所以，在 Discuss both these views and give your own opinion 的这类题目中，你可以使用 Conclusion 结论，但是在 To what extent do you agree or disagree 这种题型中则不能使用。

▶ **Is this a positive or negative development? 这是一个积极的还是消极的发展趋势？**

Similarly to the 'To what extent …' essays, you don't necessarily need to write about both sides of the statement. You first need to think about your answer to the question, and then give two reasons why; one in each paragraph, and finish off with a Conclusion.

类似于 To what extent … 这类题型，你不一定要写出陈述的正反两面。首先你需要思考你的答案，然后给出两个理由，每个段落写一个，最后写出结论。

The overall structure is similar to the previous two question types:

这类题型的作文结构与之前两种题型非常相似：

| Introduction<br>开头段 | Rewriting the initial statement and indicating the plan of your essay.<br>重申题目观点并表明你的文章内容计划。 |
| --- | --- |
| Main Body Paragraph 1<br>主体段第 1 段 | 1st reason for your position, and an example.<br>支持你的观点的第一个理由并举例。 |
| Main Body Paragraph 2<br>主体段第 2 段 | 2nd reason for your position, and an example.<br>支持你的观点的第二个理由并举例。 |
| Conclusion<br>结论 | Whether you think it's Positive or Negative and why.<br>重申你认为这是积极的还是消极的并说明原因。 |

Sometimes this kind of question is worded slightly differently, so it changes to Advantages and Disadvantages. The meaning of this is very slightly different to Positive and Negative. An example from modern times would be AI; an advantage may be that it can answer students' questions in a natural way. This isn't a positive development if you want to be a teacher.

有时这类题目的措辞会略有不同，比如换成：Advantages and Disadvantages（优点和缺点）。这种提问与 Positive and Negative 有一点区别。一个典型的例子就是关于 AI 的题目，优点就是 AI 可能会用自然的方式回答学生的问题，但如果你想成为一名教师，这并不是一个积极的发展趋势。

## ▶ Other question types 其他题型

These last types of questions can vary enormously, quite often come in twos (but not always) and can literally be anything. For example, the questions for the 'Other' Task 2 essays that appear later in this book are below:

其他这几类题型可能差异很大，常常会两种类型放在一起（但不总是如此），也可能会是任何类型。例如，在本书后面列出的 Task 2 "其他" 类型题目的例子如下：

*Why do you think organisations are introducing these special days?*
*How effective can these days be?*

*What do you think are the causes of this problem?*
*What measures could be taken to solve it?*

These typically ask you to write more of a cause/effect essay rather than an argumentative one. The principal approach to this is still to understand precisely what is being asked and then to give the answer directly. One of the advantages of this essay style is that it allows you to easily structure your essay because the first question is answered in the first paragraph and the following question in the second paragraph. Surround these paragraphs with your Introduction and Summary, and Hey, presto!

you have a complete essay.

这类题目要求你写更倾向因果关系的文章，而不是议论型的文章。主要解决方法仍然是，要先准确地理解题目的要求，然后直接作答。这类题目的一大优点就是你的行文结构会比较容易，第 1 个问题在主体段第 1 段回答，第 2 个问题在主体段第 2 段回答。再加上开头段与结尾段。嘿，转眼之间！你就完成整篇作文了。

# Chapter 2 Question Types and Sample Answers
## 题目类型及答案范例

## ■ Discuss both these views and give your opinion.

Example 1 *Question and Answer*

*You should spend about 40 minutes on this task.*

*Write about the following topic:*

> **Some people think that newspapers are the best way to learn about the news. Others, however, believe that they can learn about the news more effectively through other media.**
>
> **Discuss both these views and give your opinion.**

*Give reasons for your answer and include any relevant examples from your own knowledge or experience.*

*Write at least 250 words.*

Some believe that newspapers still are the best way to read and learn about current affairs, whereas others think that the new forms of media have now replaced them. The following essay will describe both sides of this argument and explain why I believe that newspapers are still worthy of our time.

On the one hand, newspapers have been the primary source of news for decades, and although technology seems to be replacing them, many people do not have access to modern smartphones or computers or cannot, or simply do not want, to use them. A perfect example of this is my 80-year-old grandfather. Although he finally has a HUAWEI and access to the Internet, he still obtains great tactile pleasure from a newspaper.

On the other hand, the younger generation and certainly the millennials have never really experienced newspapers in the modern world. The proliferation of new media, from TV to the Internet, has overwhelmed the need for printed materials. Even some of the poorest developing countries now have faster, more up-to-date ways of disseminating information. Take India as an example, 20 years ago, the Internet did not really exist, and only a few households had TVs. But, although this number has increased dramatically, it does not cover everyone.

In conclusion, although newspapers have certainly taken a hit on their particular form of media, I firmly believe that there will always be those that prefer to hold one in their hands in order to obtain news, as well as those that are unable to access any other form, at least for the foreseeable future.

***Word Count: 265***

有些人认为报纸仍是阅读和了解时事的最佳途径，而另一些人则认为新媒体形式已取代报纸。下面这篇文章将描述这场争论的两个方面，并解释为什么我认为报纸仍值得我们花时间阅读。

一方面，数十年来，报纸一直是新闻的主要来源，尽管采用高科技的新媒体形式似乎正在取代报纸，但仍有许多人没有使用现代智能手机或电脑的机会——或者不能使用或只是不想使用。我那年满80岁的祖父就是一个很好的例子。尽管他终于拥有一部华为手机并能上网，但他仍从触摸报纸中获得巨大的乐趣。

另一方面，年轻一代，当然还有千禧一代，从来没有真正体验过现代世界的报纸。从电视到互联网，新媒体不断激增，导致人们对印刷材料的需求大大减少。甚至一些最贫穷的发展中国家现在也有了更快、更先进的信息传播方式。以印度为例，20年前，确实还不存在互联网，只有少数印度家庭拥有电视。但是，尽管拥有电视的印度家庭数量急剧增加，但这一趋势并未覆盖所有人。

总之，虽然报纸作为一种特殊媒体形式的确受到冲击，但我坚信，至少在不久的将来，总有一些人更喜欢拿着报纸来获取新闻，也有一些人无法有机会使用任何其他形式的媒体。

## Example 1  *Approach*

### ▶ Question Keywords 题目关键词

newspapers → best way to learn news

other media more effective → other people

### ▶ Ideas 构思

other media → TikTok, Facebook, TV, Radio

use Grandpa for Newspaper, Me for 'other' media

GP can't use a computer, Me = Internet

| Examiner's Comment | | | |
|---|---|---|---|
| Coherence and Cohesion | Logical | ☑ | |
| | Progression | On the one hand, On the other hand, In conclusion | ☑ |
| Lexical Resource | Range | best way, primary source | ☑ |
| | Less Common | proliferation, disseminating, foreseeable | ☑ |
| Grammatical Range and Accuracy | Simple Structures | ☑ | |
| | Complex Structures | ☑ | |

Example 2　*Question and Answer*

*You should spend about 40 minutes on this task.*

*Write about the following topic:*

> **Lectures were used in the past as a way of teaching large numbers of students. With the technology now available for education, there is no longer any justification for this way of teaching.**
>
> **Discuss both these views and give your opinion.**

*Give reasons for your answer and include any relevant examples from your own knowledge or experience.*

*Write at least 250 words.*

Over the last few years, technology has advanced to a point where it can be used for educational purposes to replace certain teaching styles, namely large lectures performed in theatres. Some people believe that because of these advancements, there is now no reason to have people implement this way of learning.

On the one hand, Internet speeds now allow for stable international and domestic video conferencing. Recently, the need for classes and lectures performed in this way has risen around the world and with apps like Zoom, Teams, and Tencent Meeting have become a popular and somewhat trusted method of education, albeit only available in countries/cities with good Internet connection.

On the other hand, many students, of which I am one, much prefer face-to-face communication with a teacher. Many times when a large number of students attend the online meeting, I have had connection problems, which can affect both audio and video reception. In addition, teachers invariably are unfamiliar with the technologies they are being asked to use, so again, the issues affect the quality of communication from teachers to students.

Overall, I believe that technology can indeed help teachers with their lectures but in a more supportive role rather than trying to replace them. There is a significant difference between being able to use something and whether you should use something. In my opinion, this goes for relatively simple technology like video conferencing or the more advanced elements like the new Artificial Technologies (AI) like ChatGPT that have been developed more recently.

***Word Count: 253***

在过去几年里，科技已发展到可用于教育目的来取代某些教学方式的地步，即在阶梯式教室里进行的大型讲座式授课。有些人认为，由于这些科技进步，现在没有理由让人们采用上述这种学习方式。

一方面，互联网速度现在允许进行效果稳定的国际和国内视频会议。最近，世界各地对以这种方式进行的班级式授课和讲座式授课的需求不断增加，通过 Zoom、Teams 和腾讯会议等应用程序，这种教育方式已成为一种受欢迎和有些可信的方式，尽管它只在互联网连接良好的国家或城市可用。

另一方面，许多学生包括我本人在内，更喜欢与老师面对面交流。很多时候，当有大量学生参加在线会议时，我遇到过网络连接问题，而这可能会影响音频和视频接收。此外，老师总是不熟悉他们被要求使用的新媒体技术，因此，这些问题再次影响老师与学生之间的交流质量。

总体而言，我认为科技确实可以帮助老师授课，但更多的是支持性作用，而不是试图取代老师。能够使用某项事物和是否应使用某项事物之间的区别很大。在我看来，这个观点适用于相对简单的技术，例如视频会议，或者更高级的元素，如最近开发的新人工技术（人工智能）（如 ChatGPT）。

## Example 2  *Approach*

▶ **Question Keywords** 题目关键词

lectures, large numbers of students

technology, no... justification for teaching

▶ **Ideas** 构思

pro – Online classes available through Zoom/Tencent Meeting

against – Students prefer to have 'in-person lectures'

| Examiner's Comment | | | |
|---|---|---|---|
| Coherence and Cohesion | Logical | ☑ | |
| | Progression | On the one hand, On the other hand, In addition | ☑ |
| Lexical Resource | Range | teaching, performed, way of learning | ☑ |
| | Less Common | domestic, albeit, significant | ☑ |
| Grammatical Range and Accuracy | Simple Structures | ☑ | |
| | Complex Structures | ☑ | |

Example 3 *Question and Answer*

*You should spend about 40 minutes on this task.*

*Write about the following topic:*

> **Some people say that all mobile/cell phone conversations should be banned in public and crowded places. Others disagree.**
>
> **Discuss both these views and give your opinion.**

*Give reasons for your answer and include any relevant examples from your own knowledge or experience.*

*Write at least 250 words.*

To ban the mobile phone in public, or not to ban it? That seems to be the question that divides many people in modern society. The following essay will describe each side of this hotly debated topic and also give my thoughts on the situation.

To begin with, I would like to look at the modern generation that feels it is OK to use mobile phones in public places, of which I am one. Firstly, it is not possible to dictate the time when you will, or will not, receive a phone call. It may be pretty early in the morning or quite late at night, and you can almost guarantee that there will be several during 'working hours', and at all of these times, depending on your job, you could be surrounded by people. Therefore, in my view, it is not whether these conversations should be prohibited but whether they can be answered respectfully. For example, receiving a phone call in a hospital could be picked up quietly in the ward and then taken outside for a more detailed, potentially loud, conversation.

Some feel answering a call is an invasion of their privacy and causes too much noise pollution. Not only that, but they get infuriated by it much faster than, say, a dog barking on a walk with its owner. I can appreciate the need for quiet at times, certainly on a commute in the morning, as an example, and firmly believe that creating quiet zones is a wonderful idea. Still, modern technology is a 24/7/365 concept, and these days people from different countries communicate all the time.

Overall, in my opinion, I think that it is the older people from previous generations that find this troublesome. These days we consider it part of life and, to be perfectly honest, are used to tuning it out. People speaking into Bluetooth headsets or on their phones anywhere and everywhere are now merely part of life.

**Word Count: 326**

是否要在公共场合禁用手机？这似乎是现代社会中许多人存在分歧的问题。下面这篇文章将描述这个热议话题的各个方面，并给出我对这种情况的想法。

我想先看看认为可以在公共场所使用手机的现代一族，我也是其中一员。首先，你不可能规定何时会接到电话，何时不会接到电话。接电话的时间可能是清晨，也可能是深夜，同时你几乎可以肯定在"工作时间"会接到几个电话，在所有这些时间里，你可能身边围着很多人，具体情况视你的工作性质而定。因此，在我看来，不是是否应禁止这些对话，而是能否尊重地回答这些对话。例如，在医院里接到电话时，可在病房里轻声地接起电话，之后将电话带到外面进行更详细、可能更大声的对话。

有些人觉得有人在公共场所接电话会干扰他们的清静生活，还会造成太多的噪音污染。不仅如此，此举激怒他们的速度比一条狗在和主人散步时狂吠要快得多。我能理解人们有时需要安静的环境，比如在早上通勤的时候，我坚信营造安静的区域是个好主意。尽管如此，现代科技是一个"全年无休"的概念，因为如今来自不同国家的人一直在交流。

总体而言，在我看来，我认为是上一代的老年人觉得在公共场所使用手机会引起麻烦。如今我们认为手机是生活的一部分，老实说，习惯于忽视手机。现在人们在任何地方对着蓝牙耳机或手机说话都只是生活的一部分。

## Example 3  *Approach*

### ▶ Question Keywords 题目关键词

mobile/cell phone banned

public and crowded places

### ▶ Ideas 构思

timing of phone calls, modern generation

noise pollution

| Examiner's Comment | | | |
|---|---|---|---|
| Coherence and Cohesion | Logical | ☑ | |
| | Progression | To begin with, Not only that, Overall | ☑ |
| Lexical Resource | Range | ban, prohibited; public, surrounded by people | ☑ |
| | Less Common | debated, prohibited, respectfully | ☑ |
| Grammatical Range and Accuracy | Simple Structures | ☑ | |
| | Complex Structures | ☑ | |

Example 4    *Question and Answer*

*You should spend about 40 minutes on this task.*

*Write about the following topic:*

> **Some people say that supermarkets and manufacturers have a responsibility to reduce the amount of packaging on the products they sell. Others say that it is the responsibility of the consumers to avoid buying products which have a lot of packaging.**
>
> **Discuss both these views and give your opinion.**

*Give reasons for your answer and include any relevant examples from your own knowledge or experience.*

*Write at least 250 words.*

One of the more recent environmental topics that have been discussed is who has responsibility for product packaging, those that make it and sell it or those that buy it. The following essay will go to both sides of this dilemma and explain why I believe the manufacturers/sellers should be responsible for reducing the quantity of product packaging.

Looking initially at the consumers. When people buy a product, whether this be a loaf of bread or a smartphone, do not have any choice about how much packaging is used. They can choose not to buy a particular product if they feel that the producers use too much. Still, in my opinion, this is an unlikely circumstance as most people either will not even think about the packaging quantity or, if they do, will not be too bothered about it.

Looking at the flip side of this situation, I believe that, as it is the manufacturers and supermarkets that are selling the products and either buying it from suppliers or creating it themselves, they should be the ones that have a duty to reduce, as much as possible, any packaging and certainly if it is plastic. Some companies have already made moves to limit the amount of superfluous space to reduce the waste it creates.

Overall, I do firmly believe that the companies that produce and sell all the packaging should be responsible for limiting the waste packing that enters the environment rather than the consumer, as they have no control over the amount used.

**Word Count: 254**

最近讨论的一个环境话题是谁应对产品包装负责，是制造商和卖方还是买方？下面这篇文章将从这个艰难选择的两个方面来解释为什么我认为制造商或卖方应负责减少产品包装数量。

首先看看消费者的情况。当人们购买一件产品时，无论是一个面包还是一部智能手机，均无法选择使用多少包装。如果他们觉得生产商使用太多包装，他们可以选择不购买某种特定产品。不过，我认为，这是一种不太可能出现的情况，因为大多数人甚至不会考虑包装数量，或者如果他们考虑包装数量，也不会对此太在意。

从这种情况的另一面来看，我认为，由于是制造商和超市在销售产品，或者从供应商处购买产品，或者自主制造产品，他们应该有责任尽可能减少使用任何包装，当然是减少塑料包装的使用。一些公司已经采取措施限制多余空间的数量，以减少其造成的浪费。

总的来说，我坚信生产和销售所有包装的公司应该负责限制进入环境的废弃包装，而不是要求消费者对此负责，因为他们无法控制包装的使用量。

## Example 4 *Approach*

### ▶ Question Keywords 题目关键词

supermarkets and manufacturers, responsibility, reduce packaging

others say consumers shouldn't buy products with lots of packaging

### ▶ Ideas 构思

consumers – don't think about it, or don't care

manufactures – their responsibility as they create it

| | Examiner's Comment | | |
|---|---|---|---|
| Coherence and Cohesion | Logical | ☑ | |
| | Progression | Looking initially at, Looking at the flip side, Overall | ☑ |
| Lexical Resource | Range | quantity, how much, amount | ☑ |
| | Less Common | environmental, flip side, superfluous | ☑ |
| Grammatical Range and Accuracy | Simple Structures | ☑ | |
| | Complex Structures | ☑ | |

**Example 5**  *Question and Answer*

*You should spend about 40 minutes on this task.*

*Write about the following topic:*

> **Some people think individuals are more and more dependent on each other, while others believe we are more and more independent.**
>
> **Discuss both these views and give your opinion.**

*Give reasons for your answer and include any relevant examples from your own knowledge or experience.*

*Write at least 250 words.*

There are those that believe that we, as individuals, are becoming more dependent on each other, whereas others think the opposite trend is happening. I believe that the interconnectedness of people is primarily based on the culture that you grew up in, and I will compare my knowledge about India and the UK.

In India, people, and especially families, are very close to each other, much more so than in many Western countries. It is believed that relying on others for help is a natural and normal thing. For example, many families depend on grandparents to help raise children. This is sometimes because both parents need to work, but also because the family wants to include them. So, the dependence is undoubtedly there, but it always has been and, in my view, has not actually increased.

In a country like the UK, it is my understanding that people from a very young age are taught to be more independent. I believe that because of this, people learn to 'stand on their own two feet' and believe that is the preferred way of social interaction. Using my example of grandparents raising a child. English grandparents may help on occasion with some babysitting and the like but won't help in the actual raising of the child. Again, I believe that this has been the case for many years and is inbuilt to the English traditions.

In conclusion, I do not believe that levels of dependence have increased or decreased. However, I think there are differences in the attitudes towards whether dependence or independence should change and is a good or bad thing.

***Word Count: 270***

有些人认为，作为个体，我们正变得越来越相互依赖，而另一些人则认为我们正变得越来越独立。我认为人们之间的相互联系主要基于你在成长过程中所感受的文化，我将针对我对印度和英国的了解进行比较。

在印度，人们，尤其是家庭成员彼此之间非常亲近，其亲近程度比许多西方国家要高得多。印度人认为依靠别人的帮助是一件自然且正常的事情。例如，许多家庭依靠祖父母或外祖父母帮助养育孩子。有时是因为父母双方都需要工作，但也是因为整个家庭希望祖父母或外祖父母参与分工。因此，这种依赖性无疑是存在的，但在我看来，这种依赖性一直存在，实际上并没有增加。

在像英国这样的国家，据我所知，英国人从很小的时候就被教导要更加独立。我认为正因为如此，英国人学会了"自立"，并认为这是社会交往的首选方式。以我祖父母养育孩子的事情为例。在英国，祖父母可能有时会帮忙照看孩子等等，但不会帮助承担孩子的实际养育工作。此外，我认为这种情况已经持续了很多年，并且是英国传统的一部分。

总之，我不认为人们之间的依赖程度有所增加或减少。然而，我认为对于依赖或独立是否应该改变以及是好事还是坏事的态度是不同的。

## Example 5  *Approach*

> **Question Keywords** 题目关键词

individuals more dependent or
more independent

> **Ideas** 构思

depends on culture
1st culture = India
2nd culture = UK

| | Examiner's Comment | | |
|---|---|---|---|
| Coherence and Cohesion | Logical | ☑ | |
| | Progression | India and the UK, In India, In... the UK, In conclusion | ☑ |
| Lexical Resource | Range | others, people; relying on, depend on | ☑ |
| | Less Common | interconnectedness, primarily, undoubtedly | ☑ |
| Grammatical Range and Accuracy | Simple Structures | ☑ | |
| | Complex Structures | ☑ | |

Example 6  *Question and Answer*

*You should spend about 40 minutes on this task.*

*Write about the following topic:*

> **Some people think the government should pay for healthcare and education, but others believe it is not the government's responsibility.**
>
> **Discuss both these views and give your opinion.**

*Give reasons for your answer and include any relevant examples from your own knowledge or experience.*

*Write at least 250 words.*

The discussion of whether the state or individuals should be responsible for health and education fees is still raging. I will look at both sides of this argument and explain why I believe that it is up to individuals to pay for these services but the government to manage them, as it is in many countries of the world.

Firstly, looking at health, there are many countries where the government subsidises health for its citizens. In some countries, health care is 'free' for all. In some countries, it is heavily subsidised. What's sometimes forgotten, or at least overlooked, is that the working population pays taxes and that these taxes often find their way into general population services, such as public healthcare or subsidies. So, whereas people think that governments are paying for these services, it is actually the working individuals. This does not include private healthcare, which should be paid by the individual no matter what.

Secondly, looking at education services, the same facts apply. Namely that the government gets its money from the working population and then offers, in this case, schools. From my understanding, where countries differ is the amount of 'free' education that is offered. Looking at the UK and Germany as examples, the UK offers it to 18 whereas in Germany it is 19.

In conclusion then, the debate is actually moot. Whichever way it is looked at, each of us pays for the state-run healthcare and education services. If they then wish to pay more for private hospitals or schools, then that is a choice they can make on their own.

***Word Count: 266***

关于医疗和教育费用应该由国家还是个人负责的讨论仍然十分激烈。我将从正反两方面来看待这场争论，并解释我认为应该像世界上许多国家一样由个人来支付医疗和教育服务费用，但由政府来管理相关费用的原因。

第一，在医疗方面，有许多国家的政府为其公民提供医疗补贴。在一些国家，所有人都能享用"免费"医疗保健。在一些国家，人们可以获得高额的医疗补贴。人们有时会忘记，或者至少会忽视的是，劳动人口需要纳税，而这些税收通常会用于一般的人口服务，例如公共医疗保健或补贴。因此，尽管人们认为政府支付这些服务的费用，但实际上该费用的支付者是工作的个人。这不包括私人医疗保健，因为其相关费用无论如何都应由个人支付。

第二，在教育服务方面，情况也相同。即政府从劳动人口处获得资金，之后在这种情况下给学校提供资金。在我看来，各国的不同之处在于所提供"免费"教育的程度。以英国和德国为例，英国提供18岁之前的免费教育，而德国提供19岁之前的免费教育。

总之，这场辩论没有实际意义。无论从哪个角度看，我们每个人都要为国家的医疗保健和教育服务付费。如果他们希望选择私立医院或学校，之后支付更多费用，那是他们可以自己做出的选择。

## Example 6 *Approach*

### ❯ Question Keywords 题目关键词

government pay for healthcare and education

others, not their responsibility

### ❯ Ideas 构思

government paying is actually individuals through taxes

people can pay for 'private' health and schools in addition

| Examiner's Comment | | | |
|---|---|---|---|
| Coherence and Cohesion | Logical | ☑ | |
| | Progression | Firstly, Secondly, In conclusion | ☑ |
| Lexical Resource | Range | individual, each of us | ☑ |
| | Less Common | citizens, subsidised, overlooked | ☑ |
| Grammatical Range and Accuracy | Simple Structures | ☑ | |
| | Complex Structures | ☑ | |

Example 7 *Question and Answer*

*You should spend about 40 minutes on this task.*

*Write about the following topic:*

> **Some people think hosting major international sporting events brings a lot of advantages to a country, while others believe there are more disadvantages.**
>
> **Discuss both these views and give your opinion.**

*Give reasons for your answer and include any relevant examples from your own knowledge or experience.*

*Write at least 250 words.*

Many people believe that hosting an international sporting event brings more advantages than disadvantages to the host country, others disagree. Looking at both sides of this argument, I will attempt to explain why I believe that, overall, the pros outweigh the cons.

Starting with the advantages, one of the biggest that I can think of is the fact that whatever country is the host of something like the Olympics, or the Football World Cup will have a sharp increase in the number of tourists that then visit that country, not to mention the hundreds or potentially thousands of athletes that will compete. This gives the relevant economy a huge boost that, hopefully, will be in excess of the costs associated with the event, as well as the ability to allow other countries of the world to see that country in a favourable light that could open up more opportunities in the future.

The costs can be looked at as one of the most significant disadvantages. Many people of the host country could believe that the money being spent on winning the initial bid and then on the new infrastructure is better used on health or education services, or other things that would directly and immediately help its own population.

To conclude, I firmly believe that investing in sporting events can be profitable not only for the event itself, through tourism and trade, but also through future trade and tourism opportunities that may arise. This can occasionally be unpopular with the local population in the short term, but invariably the relevant people have made the calculations for the country's long-term economic benefit.

***Word Count: 271***

许多人认为举办国际体育赛事给主办国带来的好处多于坏处，其他人则不同意此观点。从这场争论的正反两方面来看待，我将试图解释为什么我认为总的来说举办国际体育赛事对主办国而言利大于弊。

首先谈及好处，我能想到的一项最大好处是，无论哪个国家主办奥运会或足球世界杯等赛事，都会使前往该国的游客数量急剧增加，更不用说数百或可能数千名运动员将参加比赛。这给相关经济带来了巨大的推动力，将有望超过与该赛事相关的成本，并能够让世界其他国家以赞赏态度看待该国，从而可能在未来带来更多的机会。

成本可被视为一项最大坏处。主办国的许多人可能会认为，将花费在赢得最初投标和之后新基础设施建设上的钱用于医疗或教育服务，或其他能直接和立即帮助本国人民的事情会更好。

最后，我坚信投资体育赛事不仅可以通过旅游和贸易为赛事本身带来收益，还可以通过未来可能出现的贸易和旅游机会带来收益。这在短期内可能有时不受当地人民的欢迎，但相关人员总是为国家的长期经济利益进行衡量。

## Example 7  *Approach*

### ❯ Question Keywords 题目关键词

international sporting events, bring advantages to a country

others think more disadvantages

### ❯ Ideas 构思

advantages = tourism increase, higher profile

disadvantages = huge cost, critical press

| Examiner's Comment | | | |
|---|---|---|---|
| Coherence and Cohesion | Logical | ☑ | |
| | Progression | Starting with, To conclude | ☑ |
| Lexical Resource | Range | advantages, pros; disadvantages, cons | ☑ |
| | Less Common | outweigh, mention, infrastructure, invariably | ☑ |
| Grammatical Range and Accuracy | Simple Structures | ☑ | |
| | Complex Structures | ☑ | |

## ■ To what extent do you agree and disagree?

Example 1    *Question and Answer*

*You should spend about 40 minutes on this task.*

*Write about the following topic:*

> **People today are surrounded by all kinds of advertising. This both affects what they think is important and is a negative influence on their lives.**
>
> **To what extent do you agree or disagree?**

*Give reasons for your answer and include any relevant examples from your own knowledge or experience.*

*Write at least 250 words.*

Nowadays, everywhere you look, there is an advert for something or other, whether it is a new high-tech gadget or a new form of cosmetic. It is inescapable that society is constantly bombarded by marketing and advertising. The following essay will describe if it controls people's thoughts and negatively affects their daily life.

Initially, looking at the question of the changing mindset, I am inclined to agree with this aspect. The sheer quantity of advertising has grown exponentially over the years and is very much a part of everybody's life. In my experience, especially when using technology, such as smartphones and the Internet, I am constantly interrupted by pop-ups, adverts in apps, video adverts in games and the like. Because of the repetitiveness of it all, I can feel my opinions changing about the importance of 'keeping up with the Joneses' and ensuring I also have the latest 'HUAWEI 25XS++'.

As for whether this is a negative trend, again, I am leaning more towards Yes, than No. When I was much younger, I was more concerned with spending time with my family and friends, playing football in the playground, and which girl I fancied than the configuration of my PC at home. So, maybe age is a factor that should be considered in this equation. Having said that, in modern times, a girl might not go on a date with me unless I have up-to-date tech.

To conclude, I have to say modern advertising influences how people think and that this is indeed an undesirable trend.

***Word Count: 256***

如今，目之所及，都是各种广告，不管它推广的产品是一种新的高科技小玩意儿还是一款新的化妆品。社会不断受到营销和广告的轰炸是不可避免的。下面这篇文章将描述这种情况是否控制了人们的思想，并对他们的日常生活产生了负面影响。

最初，我倾向于同意会带来思维转变这一方面。这些年来，广告的数量呈指数增长，已经成为每个人生活非常重要的一部分。根据我的经验，特别是在使用智能手机和互联网等技术时，我经常会被弹窗、应用程序中的广告、游戏中的视频广告等打断。由于广告的重复性，我可以感觉到我对"与他人攀比"和确保我也拥有最新的"华为 25XS++"手机系列重要性的看法正在发生变化。

至于这是否是一种负面趋势，我还是倾向于表示肯定，而不是否定。在我年轻的时候，我更关心的是与家人和朋友共度时光，在操场上踢足球，以及我喜欢哪个女孩，而不是我家里的个人电脑的配置。因此，也许年龄是这个复杂局面中应该考虑的一个因素。话虽如此，在现代，除非我拥有最新的科技产品，否则女孩可能不会和我约会。

总之，我不得不说现代广告影响了人们的思维方式，这确实是一种不良趋势。

## Example 1 *Approach*

▶ **Question Keywords** 题目关键词

advertising, affects what people think is important

negative influence

▶ **Ideas** 构思

repetitive, everywhere on smartphones

my experience as a child/teenager

| Examiner's Comment | | | |
|---|---|---|---|
| Coherence and Cohesion | Logical | ☑ | |
| | Progression | Initially, As for, To conclude | ☑ |
| Lexical Resource | Range | controls, affects, influences | ☑ |
| | Less Common | gadget, repetitiveness, factor | ☑ |
| Grammatical Range and Accuracy | Simple Structures | ☑ | |
| | Complex Structures | ☑ | |

Example 2　*Question and Answer*

*You should spend about 40 minutes on this task.*

*Write about the following topic:*

> **Sending criminals to prison is not an effective method of dealing with them. Education and job training should be used instead.**
>
> **To what extent do you agree or disagree?**

*Give reasons for your answer and include any relevant examples from your own knowledge or experience.*

*Write at least 250 words.*

The belief that prison is not a good way of dealing with the criminal element of society is not universal. Some believe that they should be offered learning opportunities and training instead. The following essay will describe why I completely disagree with this standpoint.

Firstly, criminals are not desired members of society. They are neither needed, nor wanted. When a person decides to commit a crime, for whatever reason, it is a conscious choice that either harms an organisation or another person deliberately and should be punished accordingly. Someone who commits murder, for example, has taken the life of another human being. This cannot be reversed and does irreparable damage to the victim's family concerned. The idea that they could be educated and become a contributing member of society is laughable.

Secondly, a large percentage of people that turn to crime in the first place are uneducated. If this was not the case, why would they turn to crime in the first place? Trying to educate a person who has already proven that they are unteachable seems like a waste of time and effort with no guarantee of success.

In conclusion, I firmly believe that criminals, having committed whatever crime, should be punished and removed from society for the length of time deemed correct by the courts. Should the offence be a capital one, then there is only one punishment I believe is appropriate: capital punishment. Anything else would be offensive to the victims and/or their families, not to mention society as a whole.

***Word Count: 254***

认为监禁不是处理社会犯罪分子的好方法的想法并不普遍。一些人认为应该为他们提供学习机会和培训。下面这篇文章将描述我完全不同意这个观点的原因。

第一，罪犯不是想要的社会成员。社会既不需要，也不想要他们。当一个人决定犯罪时，无论出于何种原因，这都是一种有意识的选择，无论是故意伤害一个组织还是故意伤害另一个人，相关罪犯都应该受到相应的惩罚。例如，有人犯了谋杀罪，夺走了另一个人的生命。这种情况是不可逆转的，对受害者的有关家庭造成了无法挽回的损害。认为他们可以接受教育并成为对社会有贡献的一员的想法很可笑。

第二，很大一部分走上犯罪道路的人原先没有受过教育。如果他们受过教育，为什么他们原先会走上犯罪的道路？试图教育一个已经证明他们是不可教的人似乎是浪费时间和精力，而且不能保证成功。

总之，我坚信无论犯了什么罪的罪犯都应该受到惩罚，并在法庭认为合适的时长进行监禁。如果是死罪，那么我认为只有一种惩罚合适：死刑。其他任何惩罚都会触怒受害者和（或）他们的家人，更不用说整个社会了。

## Example 2  *Approach*

▶ **Question Keywords 题目关键词**

criminals, prison not effective

education, training should be used

▶ **Ideas 构思**

criminals = not needed/wanted, can't educate the unteachable

| Examiner's Comment | | | |
|---|---|---|---|
| Coherence and Cohesion | Logical | ☑ | |
| | Progression | Firstly, Secondly, In conclusion | ☑ |
| Lexical Resource | Range | murder, taken the life | ☑ |
| | Less Common | standpoint, deliberately, commits, guarantee | ☑ |
| Grammatical Range and Accuracy | Simple Structures | ☑ | |
| | Complex Structures | ☑ | |

**Example 3** *Question and Answer*

*You should spend about 40 minutes on this task.*

*Write about the following topic:*

> **The tendency for news reports in the media to focus on problems and emergencies rather than on positive developments is harmful to the individual and to society.**
>
> **To what extent do you agree or disagree?**

*Give reasons for your answer and include any relevant examples from your own knowledge or experience.*

*Write at least 250 words.*

Historically, news reports in Western countries have only reported mostly negative elements rather than the positive ones and, by some, is considered harmful to both a person and a people. I completely agree with this point of view, and the following essay will describe my reasons why this is the case.

From my own experience of watching or reading current affairs, whether this be from a TV, newspaper or even on the Internet, it has always seemed that the world is falling apart. The news appears to be very focused on crime, war, disasters or, more recently, trade conflict, the bad things that are happening in the world, with very little in the way of uplifting stories to counter the negative feelings that this produces.

The result of this is that people have negative thoughts and emotions about the world and those that live in it, beyond their own social circle. This, to my mind, can not be avoided and is both harmful and detrimental to all concerned. A clear example of this would be the stories about nationalism and trade wars. All countries believe what they are doing is in the best interests of their country, but it has undoubtedly soured their relations. It has caused lots of regular people to doubt each other and can lead to mistrust.

In conclusion, the news is a powerful medium and is often the only source of information for a person or people. The fact that they are constantly bombarded by 'bad' news will, in my view, harm not only relations between countries but also individuals and create a negative circle that would be hard to break.

***Word Count: 275***

从历史上来看，西方国家的新闻报道大多只报道负面事件，而不是正面事件，有些人认为这种情况对一个人和一个民族都有害。我完全同意这个观点，下面这篇文章将描述我同意这个观点的原因。

从我自己观看或阅读时事的经验来看，无论是来自电视、报纸，或者甚至是互联网，世界似乎总是在分崩离析。新闻似乎非常关注犯罪、战争、灾难，或者最近发生的贸易冲突，以及世界上正在发生的坏事，却很少报道令人振奋的新闻报道来抵消由此产生的负面情绪。

新闻只报道负面事件所产生的结果是，人们对他们自己的社交圈之外的这个世界以及生活在这个世界的人有负面的想法和情绪。我认为这种情况是不可避免的，而且对所有相关的人都有害。一个明显的例子是关于民族主义和贸易战的新闻。所有国家都认为他们所做的事情符合他们国家的最大利益，但这无疑恶化了国家间的关系。这导致许多普通人互相怀疑，并可能导致不信任。

总之，新闻是一种强有力的媒体，通常是一个人或一个民族唯一的信息来源。我认为，他们不断被"坏"消息轰炸不仅会损害国家间的关系，也会损害个人，并形成一个难以打破的负面循环。

## Example 3 *Approach*

> **Question Keywords** 题目关键词

news reports focus problems not on positive things = harmful to individuals and society

> **Ideas** 构思

confirm negative news

spreads negative feeling and emotions

| Examiner's Comment | | | |
|---|---|---|---|
| Coherence and Cohesion | Logical | ☑ | |
| | Progression | The result of this, In conclusion | ☑ |
| Lexical Resource | Range | negative, harmful, detrimental | ☑ |
| | Less Common | uplifting, relations, mistrust | ☑ |
| Grammatical Range and Accuracy | Simple Structures | ☑ | |
| | Complex Structures | ☑ | |

Example 4 *Question and Answer*

*You should spend about 40 minutes on this task.*

*Write about the following topic:*

> **Lectures were used in the past as a way of teaching large numbers of students. With the technology now available for education, there is no longer any justification for this way of teaching.**
>
> **To what extent do you agree or disagree?**

*Give reasons for your answer and include any relevant examples from your own knowledge or experience.*

*Write at least 250 words.*

The statement suggests that with the current level of technology available in the educational industry, 'lectures' are no longer necessary to teach large numbers of students. The following essay will explain why I think that this is utter nonsense.

To begin with, I would like to look at the technology that is available to the teaching profession. PCs with Powerpoint installed, attached to a projector, are what instantly comes to mind as has been used in my university ever since I began there. Although video conferencing is still being used, and is remote, does not change the approach and style of presentation, namely Teacher and PPT, with students listening, or at least pretending to.

Progressing onto the 'Lecture' format and the definition of 'large numbers' of students. The 'classes' I have attended generally have around 30 students, with lectures ranging from 50 or 60 to 300 or 400, so the numbers are somewhat different. With this number of students, a teacher cannot hope to pay any kind of personal attention to a student and therefore performs his/her lecture on stage and then maybe has time for a Q&A at the end. This style is used irrespective of location, audience, and technology. It can be done in an open-air park, a university hall or on Zoom, it really does not matter. What does matter is that the students receive the information.

In conclusion, I firmly believe that the 'lecture' style is here to stay, and although the introduction of technology can assist in reaching more students at one time (like Zoom), I do not think this technology will replace a tried and tested, and expected, method of education.

***Word Count: 277***

题目表明，在教育行业现有的技术水平下，"讲座式授课"不再是教授大量学生的必要手段。下面这篇文章将解释我认为这完全是胡说八道的原因。

首先，我想看看教育行业可用的技术。将安装有Powerpoint软件的个人电脑连接到投影仪上，是我第一时间想到的相关技术，自从我读大学开始，就一直在使用它。虽然视频会议仍在使用，而且是远程会议，但并没有改变课程演示的方式和风格，即教师和PPT，同时学生在听课，或者至少假装在听课。

再到"讲座式授课"形式和"大量"学生的定义。我所上过的"班级式授课"的学生人数一般有30人左右，而参加讲座式授课的学生人数从50或60人到300或400人不等，因此两种授课方式的学生人数有些不同。面对如此多的学生，老师不可能希望对学生给予任何形式的个人关注，因此他或她会在台上讲课，然后可能在最后会有时间进行问答。这种风格的使用不受地点、对象和技术的影响。可以在露天公园、大学礼堂或者用Zoom软件讲课，这真的都不重要。重要的是学生能接收教师所传达的信息。

总之，我坚信"讲座式授课"风格将会继续存在，尽管技术的引入可以帮助同时教授更多的学生（如Zoom软件），但我认为这种技术将不会取代久经考验且符合预期的教育方法。

## Example 4 *Approach*

▶ **Question Keywords** 题目关键词

past lectures can teach lots of students

technology = no need for lectures

▶ **Ideas** 构思

technology = PPT, projector; now = video conferencing

lecture style, numbers of students

| | | Examiner's Comment | |
|---|---|---|---|
| Coherence and Cohesion | Logical | ☑ | |
| | Progression | To begin with, Progressing onto, In conclusion | ☑ |
| Lexical Resource | Range | lectures, teach, education | ☑ |
| | Less Common | nonsense, profession, projector, Progressing, irrespective | ☑ |
| Grammatical Range and Accuracy | Simple Structures | ☑ | |
| | Complex Structures | ☑ | |

*Important Information:* *You may have noticed that this topic was used earlier for a different style of question. Make sure that you can understand what's the same and what's different about the two essays.*

**重要信息：**你可能已经注意到，这个话题在之前被用于不同类型的问题。确保你能理解两篇文章的相同之处和不同之处。

Example 5    *Question and Answer*

*You should spend about 40 minutes on this task.*

*Write about the following topic:*

---

**The environmental problems facing today's world are so great that there is little ordinary people can do to improve the situation. Governments and large companies should be responsible for reducing the amount of damage being done to the environment.**

**To what extent do you agree or disagree?**

---

*Give reasons for your answer and include any relevant examples from your own knowledge or experience.*

*Write at least 250 words.*

The environment and what we should do about it is an ongoing issue. Who is responsible for dealing with it, the private citizen or governments and major commercial concerns?

Governments and big businesses are undoubtedly the major players but each of us private citizens undoubtedly bears some responsibility and has a role to play in alleviating this ever-increasing problem. As individuals, we need to increase our awareness of this as an issue only by realising it as a problem will we look for solutions, and in turn pressure our representatives to take action. Also, we will support fewer environmentally harmful products, so, for example, we will buy electric cars instead of the current vehicles which are powered mainly by fossil fuel products such as petrol.

State representatives must take action by making laws which we must obey. For example, in some city centres, it is illegal to let off fireworks. Also, they can make big businesses take action. In many countries, at the supermarket, we must purchase plastic bags whereas before we got them free, this action has reduced the number of plastic bags as we do not want to continually pay for a new one, so we bring an old one with us. In this way, both the citizen and businesses are controlled in a positive way.

In conclusion, I would argue that the ordinary citizen is the most important component in this dilemma, as they alone can put pressure on both the state and big business concerns and should not be underestimated.

***Word Count: 254***

环境与我们应该采取的环保措施是一个持续存在的问题。谁来负责处理这个问题，是普通公民、政府还是主要商业公司？

　　政府和大型公司无疑是环保工作的主要参与者，但我们每个普通公民无疑都负有一定责任，而且在缓解这一日益严重的环保问题方面也发挥着作用。作为个人，我们需要提高对这一环保问题的认识。只有认识到这是一个问题，我们才会寻求解决方案，进而迫使我们的代表采取行动。此外，我们将支持使用对环境危害较小的产品。例如，我们将购买电动汽车，而不是目前主要由汽油等化石燃料产品驱动的汽车。

　　国家代表必须通过制定我们必须遵守的法律来采取环保措施。例如，在一些城市中心，燃放烟花属于违法行为。此外，国家代表还可以让大型企业采取环保措施。在很多国家，我们在超市购物时必须购买塑料袋，而此前我们免费获得塑料袋，这一环保措施减少了塑料袋的使用数量，因为我们在购物时不想不断花钱买新的塑料袋，所以我们会携带一个旧的塑料袋去购物。通过这种方式，公民和企业在环保方面都受到积极管控。

　　总之，我认为普通公民是这一艰难选择中最重要的因素，因为只有他们才能对国家和大型企业施加压力，因此不得低估其能力。

## Example 5 *Approach*

### ▶ Question Keywords 题目关键词

environmental problems can't be solved by people

government and companies should be responsible

### ▶ Ideas 构思

individuals can make a difference = less harmful products, fossil fuels

government = laws; big business = supermarkets, plastic bags

| | Examiner's Comment | | |
|---|---|---|---|
| Coherence and Cohesion | Logical | ☑ | |
| | Progression | Governments and big businesses, State representatives, big businesses, In conclusion | ☑ |
| Lexical Resource | Range | private citizen, individuals | ☑ |
| | Less Common | undoubtedly, fossil fuel, representatives, dilemma | ☑ |
| Grammatical Range and Accuracy | Simple Structures | ☑ | |
| | Complex Structures | ☑ | |

Example 6    *Question and Answer*

*You should spend about 40 minutes on this task.*

*Write about the following topic:*

> **Children who find subjects such as Mathematics and Philosophy too difficult should not be made to study them at school. These subjects should be optional rather than compulsory.**
>
> **To what extent do you agree or disagree with this statement?**

*Give reasons for your answer and include any relevant examples from your own knowledge or experience.*

*Write at least 250 words.*

Children's education is often a point of contention, especially when students find particular subjects difficult. The following essay will describe why I completely disagree with the notion that just because a subject is 'hard', it should be made voluntary rather than mandatory.

Firstly, just because a subject may not be that easy to study, some, myself included, believe that that is what makes it more interesting. The fact that it is a challenge is actually part of the fun of learning. The examples given, namely Maths and Philosophy, are poles apart in my mind, but both will make you think differently. Surely that is the function of education. I won't become a philosopher in the future, but that does not mean I should not know something about it.

Secondly, I firmly believe that all STEM subjects should be obligatory, without exception. So, Mathematics should be included. Philosophy, however, I believe could be an elective. Not because it's difficult but because it might not be where the student wants to go. I know that in the UK, you can elect to study different courses at the age of 14 for GCSEs and drop others. For me at that age, I did not necessarily know what job I was going to have, but I surely knew it was not going to involve CDT, so I would have loved to be able to drop it.

In conclusion, I sincerely do not think subjects should be dropped because of the difficulty level. All subjects should be embraced to a certain level. However, it is natural that students will find some subjects more straightforward than others and may choose to focus on the ones they find easier during their educational journey.

***Word Count: 286***

孩子的教育常常是争论的焦点，尤其是在学生认为某些学科太难时会引起争论。下面这篇文章将说明为何我完全不同意仅仅因为一门学科"太难"，就应该将它变成选修课，而不是必修课。

　　第一，仅仅因为一门学科可能没那么容易学习，包括我自己在内的一些人认为这是这门学科更有趣的原因。承认这门学科是一项挑战实际上是学习乐趣的一部分。在我看来，所给的例子（即数学和哲学）的情况截然不同，但两者都会让你有不同的想法。这当然是教育的功能。我以后不会成为哲学家，但这不代表我不该了解关于哲学的一些知识。

　　第二，我坚信所有科学、技术、工程和数学（STEM）学科无一例外都应该是必修学科。因此，数学应该包括在内。然而，我认为哲学可以作为一门选修课。不是因为它很难，而是因为它可能不是学生想要接触的学科。我知道，在英国，你可以选择在14岁时为普通中等教育证书（GCSE）学习不同的课程，并放弃其他课程。对处于那个年龄的我而言，我不一定知道我将来会从事什么工作，但我肯定知道这不会涉及工艺、设计和技术（CDT）科目，所以我很希望能够放弃这门课程。

　　总之，我真诚地认为不应该因为难度而放弃学科。应该对所有学科接触到一定程度。然而，很自然，学生们会发现一些学科比其他学科更简单，并且可能会选择专注于他们在教育过程中发现更简单的学科。

---

Example 6　*Approach*

▶ **Question Keywords** 题目关键词

Maths and Philosophy

▶ **Ideas** 构思

study is for interest not career

STEM (Science, Technology, Engineering, Mathematics) should be compulsory

| Examiner's Comment | | | |
|---|---|---|---|
| Coherence and Cohesion | Logical | ☑ | |
| | Progression | Firstly, Secondly, In conclusion, However | ☑ |
| Lexical Resource | Range | ☑ | |
| | Less Common | function, involve, embraced | ☑ |
| Grammatical Range and Accuracy | Simple Structures | ☑ | |
| | Complex Structures | ☑ | |

Example 7 *Question and Answer*

*You should spend about 40 minutes on this task.*

*Write about the following topic:*

> **Many people believe that social networking sites (e.g. Facebook) have had a huge negative impact on both individuals and society.**
>
> **To what extent do you agree or disagree with this statement?**

*Give reasons for your answer and include any relevant examples from your own knowledge or experience.*

*Write at least 250 words.*

Social networking sites have become integral to most people's lives, whether they want it or not. The following essay will describe why I completely agree with the idea that they have had a wide and enormous detrimental influence on individuals and people.

To begin with, looking at the personal side of things, when apps like MSN Messenger, Skype and then Facebook, WeiBo and Twitter first emerged, they were heralded as part of the Internet 2.0 and seen to be the way forward in communication across distances. Initially, even I believed they could be good if used properly. Alas, the inevitable happened, and they became popular. So popular, in fact, that many of my co-students spend hours in a day scrolling through what I deem to be, useless and frivolous drivel. I am not interested in the fact that I must join 'this' group, or I will just be left out and not 'up with the times'. The peer pressure is enormous and, quite frankly, disturbing.

Expanding this now to the plural, whether this is a large group such as a city, or even an entire state or country, I see the same attitudes and misgivings as to the smaller-scale problems. Different countries have different ideas as to what is acceptable content, what are acceptable apps and who should be able to read what content across borders. The current disagreements between certain countries seem to illustrate this nicely. For example, some have recently banned WeChat and TikTok.

In conclusion, it seems to me that considering these apps were supposed to bring people together, they are currently doing the exact opposite. Pushing both individuals and countries further apart, not closer together. I believe that the companies are victims of their own successes and have left the rest of society as collateral damage.

***Word Count: 300***

无论是否愿意，社交网站已经成为大多数人生活中不可或缺的一部分。下面的文章将说明为何我完全同意这一观点：社交网站对个人和民族产生了广泛而巨大的不利影响。

首先，从个人角度来看，MSN Messenger、Skype、Facebook、微博和Twitter等应用程序首次出现时，就被宣称为互联网2.0的一部分，并且被视为跨越距离的通信方式。最初，即使我也这么认为，如果使用得当，它们可以发挥积极作用。唉，不可避免的事情发生了，这些应用程序逐渐受欢迎。事实上，它们太受欢迎了，以至于我的许多同学一天之中要耗费几个小时浏览我认为毫无用处、毫无意义的废话。我对我必须加入"这个"群否则我将被排除在外而无法"跟上时代"的事实不感兴趣。同龄人的压力非常大，坦率地说，这种压力令人焦虑不安。

现在问题扩展到多数范围，无论是一个大型群体，比如一个城市，还是甚至整个州或国家，我都看到对较小规模问题持有的相同态度和疑虑。关于什么是可接受的内容、什么是可接受的应用程序，以及谁应该能够跨境阅读什么内容，不同的国家有不同的观点。某些国家之间目前的分歧似乎很好地说明了这一点。比如，一些国家近期禁用了微信和抖音。

总之，在我看来，考虑到这些应用程序应该使人们团结一心，但它们目前却正在发挥完全相反的作用——将个人和国家推得更远，而不是拉近彼此的联系。我认为，这些公司是自身成功的受害者，并且给社会上的其他人都造成了附带性的损害。

## Example 7  *Approach*

### ▶ Question Keywords 题目关键词

social networks, negative impact, individuals and society

### ▶ Ideas 构思

individuals = technology way forward, became too much

society = cross-border disagreements

| Examiner's Comment | | | |
|---|---|---|---|
| Coherence and Cohesion | Logical | ☑ | |
| | Progression | To begin with, Expanding this now, In conclusion | ☑ |
| Lexical Resource | Range | individuals, personal | ☑ |
| | Less Common | inevitable, frivolous drivel, peer pressure, disturbing | ☑ |
| Grammatical Range and Accuracy | Simple Structures | ☑ | |
| | Complex Structures | ☑ | |

Example 8    *Question and Answer*

*You should spend about 40 minutes on this task.*

*Write about the following topic:*

> **When new towns are planned, it is more important to include public parks and sports facilities than shopping centres for people to spend their free time in.**
>
> **To what extent do you agree or disagree with this statement?**

*Give reasons for your answer and include any relevant examples from your own knowledge or experience.*

*Write at least 250 words.*


Planning new towns and cities is a complex process, and designs include areas where people can spend their free time. Some believe that shopping areas are essential, whereas others believe that public places like parks, gardens, or even sports facilities are more important. The following will describe why, in my opinion, they are equally important and should both be considered essential in any new development.

To begin with, shopping centres have now changed into places not only where people just buy their groceries, but also go to meet their friends and socialise. This may be simply for lunch or possibly just to meet, chat and go window shopping as my friends and I do. Personally, I find this an excellent way to relax and unwind, especially at weekends after a hard week studying or working. To me, and most of my friends, going to a park is simply dull, and the idea of sweating buckets at a gym is simply repulsive.

On the other hand, for the generations that are older than me, or even retired, I can fully understand why they would prefer a quiet place to relax away from the hustle and bustle of city life. Here in Beijing, simple exercise machines that people can use are spread out in public areas and public gardens for people to use. Therefore, while people in their spare time can relax and get some fresh air, they can also do some mild exercise, both of which are good for their health.

In conclusion, then, I do not believe that one is more important than the other. Both should have equal weight in the design phase to meet all people's needs and requirements.

***Word Count: 281***

规划新城镇和城市是一个复杂的过程，相关设计包括人们可以度过闲暇时间的片区。一些人认为购物区必不可少，而另一些人则认为公园、花园、甚至体育设施等公共场所更加重要。下面将说明为何在我看来购物区和公共场所同等重要，并且在任何新开发中都应该被视为是必不可少的。

首先，购物中心现在不仅变成人们只购买日常用品的地方，也变成了人们会见朋友和社交的地方。这可能只是用于共进午餐，也可能只是用于见面、聊天和逛街的地方，正如我和我的朋友们所做的。就我个人而言，我认为这是一个放松身心的好方法，尤其是在辛苦学习或工作一周后的周末。对我和我的大多数朋友而言，去公园太无聊，而在健身房汗流浃背的想法则令人反感。

另一方面，对于比我年长甚至已经退休的一代人而言，我完全能够理解为何他们喜欢在一个安静的地方进行放松，远离城市生活的熙攘喧嚣。在北京，人们可以使用的简单健身器械就分散摆放在公共区域和公园里，供人们使用。因此，人们在业余时间可以放松并呼吸一些新鲜空气的同时，还可以做一些轻微的运动，这两者都对健康有益。

总之，我认为购物区和公共场所的重要性不相上下。两者在设计阶段应该具有同等的重要性，以便满足所有人的需求和要求。

## Example 8  *Approach*

### ▶ Question Keywords 题目关键词

new towns, include parks and sports facilities

not shopping centres

### ▶ Ideas 构思

equally important

shopping centres not just places to buy food, socialise with friends

older generation wants quiet places, good for exercise

| Examiner's Comment | | | |
|---|---|---|---|
| Coherence and Cohesion | Logical | ☑ | |
| | Progression | To begin with, On the other hand, Therefore, In conclusion | ☑ |
| Lexical Resource | Range | socialise, window shopping, public gardens | ☑ |
| | Less Common | complex, repulsive, hustle and bustle | ☑ |
| Grammatical Range and Accuracy | Simple Structures | ☑ | |
| | Complex Structures | ☑ | |

Example 9　*Question and Answer*

*You should spend about 40 minutes on this task.*

*Write about the following topic:*

> **The news has no connection with most people's lives and it is therefore a waste of time for most of us to read newspapers and watch television news programmes.**
>
> **To what extent do you agree or disagree with this statement?**

*Give reasons for your answer and include any relevant examples from your own knowledge or experience.*

*Write at least 250 words.*

The statement in the question talks about whether the news is helpful to us in our daily lives or is simply a 'waste of time' and that we should not bother with it. Below I will describe that while I partly agree with this statement, I do not entirely agree.

I agree with the statement that some news items are solely about another area, or even country to where I live and has no relevance in my daily life. An example of this would be the recent bankruptcy of the FlyBe airline, or what the locals call 'Fly maybe'. This is specifically a UK issue with no connections to other countries. It's a short-haul airline that only flies around the UK and Europe; therefore, its collapse does not affect me, my family, or anyone else I know. It does, however, have an 'interest' value.

Other news items, though, can be of world interest and, although they may begin in one country, may have a knock-on effect on others. For example, some of the recent news about banks in the US and Europe going bankrupt. Although this happened a long way from China, it still affected the Chinese financial system, which affected my family and their finances.

In conclusion, although not all news is relevant or directly connected to me, it can be exciting and be learnt from. There is definitely some directly relevant news, which means that I should really try and keep up to date on all the elements to decide which may affect me and take appropriate steps.

***Word Count: 260***

该问题的说法谈到了新闻在我们的日常生活中是否对我们有帮助，还是只是"浪费时间"，以及我们不应该为此感到烦恼。下面我将说明，虽然我部分同意这种说法，但我对此并不完全同意。

我同意这样的说法，是因为一些新闻仅仅是关于另一个地区，甚至是关于我居住的国家，但与我的日常生活无关。这方面的一个例子是，近期英国航空公司FlyBe破产，或者当地人所说的"Fly maybe（可能飞逝）"。这是英国特有的问题，与其他国家无关。这是一家短途航空公司，只在英国和欧洲间飞行；因此，其破产并不会影响到我、我的家人或我认识的任何人。然而，这条新闻确实具有"关注"价值。

不过，其他新闻可能会引起全世界的兴趣，虽然这些新闻可能始于一个国家，但可能会对其他国家产生连锁反应。例如，近期一些关于美国和欧洲银行破产的新闻。虽然这发生在距离中国很远的地方，但它仍然影响了中国的金融体系，从而影响我的家人及其财务。

总之，虽然不是所有的新闻都与我相关或直接相关，但都可能令人振奋并从中吸取教训。当然也有一些直接相关的新闻，这意味着我应该真正尝试并了解所有最新信息，以便决定哪些可能会影响我并采取适当的应对措施。

## Example 9  *Approach*

### ▶ Question Keywords 题目关键词

news no connection to people = waste of time to read or watch news

### ▶ Ideas 构思

some news not relevant to me → FlyBe in UK

other news = international → still affects me

| | | Examiner's Comment | |
|---|---|---|---|
| Coherence and Cohesion | Logical | ☑ | |
| | Progression | I agree with, therefore, Other, Although, In conclusion | ☑ |
| Lexical Resource | Range | daily lives, relevant; another area, long way | ☑ |
| | Less Common | collapse, bankrupt, relevant | ☑ |
| Grammatical Range and Accuracy | Simple Structures | ☑ | |
| | Complex Structures | ☑ | |

# ■ Is this a positive or negative development?

Example 1   *Question and Answer*

*You should spend about 40 minutes on this task.*

*Write about the following topic:*

> **More and more people today want to buy goods, e.g. clothes and smartphones, with well-known brand names. Why is this?**
>
> **Is this a positive or negative development?**

*Give reasons for your answer and include any relevant examples from your own knowledge or experience.*

*Write at least 250 words.*


With people worldwide generally getting more affluent and the 'middle class' expanding, the desire to purchase 'well-known' brands is growing, even in developing countries. Below, I will describe the reasons for this and whether, in my humble opinion, this is a 'pro' or a 'con'.

Firstly, describing the reasons why. If a company produces a product that fills a market need and becomes popular, there is usually a good reason for this. It could be excellent design, like the HUAWEI or is just superior quality, like many of the clothing brands – LI-NING, for example. From there, their brand name grows and becomes more widespread; hence, more people want to buy them. If, for any reason, their products are not 'up to scratch', they would simply fail as businesses and never be heard of again.

Moving onto whether it is a good or bad thing – I would say, good. Primarily because I believe that if these products are popular, they must have something going for them. As I explained above, the international brand may be 'better' than the domestic one, allowing the local population to develop and grow. That is not to say that domestic brands should be forgotten entirely, but they can and should be able to improve their products to match, if not surpass, their competitors. Looking at it from this angle means that all products will develop and improve, which can only be a good thing for the consumer.

In conclusion, I see this trend towards well-known and name brands as a positive development for all concerned: the companies that make them and the customers that buy and use them.

***Word Count: 274***

随着全球人民普遍变得更加富裕,"中产阶级"规模不断扩大,对"知名"品牌的购买欲也在增长,甚至在发展中国家也是如此。下面我将说明出现这种情况的原因,以及依我拙见,这是"好事"还是"坏事"。

首先,说明相关原因。如果一家公司生产的产品满足市场需求并且受到欢迎,这通常是有原因的。其原因可能是优秀的设计,就像华为手机一样,或者只是出色的质量,就像许多服装品牌一样——例如李宁。自此,其品牌声名增长且广为人知,因此,更多的人都想要购买该品牌的产品。不管出于什么原因,如果其产品不"符合标准",则其生意就会失败,而且再也听不到该品牌。

继续讨论这是好事还是坏事,我会说这是好事。主要是因为我认为,如果这些产品受欢迎,则一定有其原因。正如我上面所解释的,国际品牌可能比国内品牌"更好",从而让当地购买人群发展壮大。这并不是说应该完全遗忘国产品牌,但国产品牌能够也应该能够改进其产品,即使不是超越其竞争对手,也能赶上其竞争对手的发展步伐。从这个角度来看,这意味着所有产品都将得到发展和改进,这对消费者而言只能是一件好事。

总之,我认为这种向知名品牌看齐的趋势对所有相关品牌、生产这些产品的公司,以及购买和使用这些产品的顾客都是一种积极的发展态势。

## Example 1 *Approach*

▶ **Question Keywords** 题目关键词

more people want brand names – why?

positive or negative?

▶ **Ideas** 构思

why = good quality products

positive = domestic can surpass international

| | | Examiner's Comment | |
|---|---|---|---|
| Coherence and Cohesion | Logical | ☑ | |
| | Progression | Firstly, Moving onto, Primarily, In conclusion | ☑ |
| Lexical Resource | Range | well-known, popular, widespread, grow | ☑ |
| | Less Common | widespread, up to scratch, domestic, surpass, concerned | ☑ |
| Grammatical Range and Accuracy | Simple Structures | ☑ | |
| | Complex Structures | ☑ | |

**Example 2** *Question and Answer*

*You should spend about 40 minutes on this task.*

*Write about the following topic:*

> **Increasing numbers of developing countries are currently expanding their tourist industries. Why is this the case?**
>
> **Is this a positive or negative development?**

*Give reasons for your answer and include any relevant examples from your own knowledge or experience.*

*Write at least 250 words.*

Countries still considered 'developing' are quickly realising that tourism is still a growth industry and that they can easily attract visitors to their mostly untouched areas to increase their economic income. I will explain why I think this is the case and why I believe this is a catastrophic situation.

It is pretty apparent why poorer countries want to grow their economies. They want to get richer and become a 'developed' nation. Countries like India, Thailand, Malaysia, and many African countries all have some of the most beautiful natural spots on the planet. Cashing in on this seems like a good idea, certainly from an economic aspect. Still, the long-term damage caused by countless visitors probably outweighs the short to medium-term gains.

*The Beach* was filmed in Thailand in the late 1990s, and since that time, this beautiful scenic spot has gotten so bad that Thai officials have now had to close it so that the area can recover from the damage caused by the enormous number of tourists that have gone there. This is merely one example; there are many others. If this trend continues due to the lack of respect for nature and the sheer number of boots hitting the ground in these places, there will be no other places of natural beauty left for anyone to enjoy.

In conclusion, because of the urgent and desperation of developing countries to 'catch up', they are destroying the places that make them unique in the first place. This is not only a negative development but also a self-destructive one.

***Word Count: 259***

仍被视为"发展中"的国家很快意识到旅游业仍然是一个增长行业，它们可以很容易地吸引游客前往其大部分未受破坏的自然地区来增加其经济收入。我将解释为何我认为情况如此，以及为何我认为这是一种灾难性的情况。

贫穷国家想要发展经济的原因显而易见。它们想要变得更富有，成为一个"发达"国家。像印度、泰国、马来西亚和许多非洲国家，它们都拥有一些地球上最美丽的自然景点。的确从经济角度来看，利用这一点来赚钱似乎是个不错的主意。尽管如此，无数游客造成的长期损害可能会超过中短期的收益。

20世纪90年代末，电影《海滩》(*The Beach*)在泰国拍摄取景，从那时起，这个美丽景点的生态环境因大量游客造访而惨遭破坏，以至于泰国官方机构现在不得不予以关闭，以便该景点能够从造访该地的大量游客所造成的破坏中恢复过来。这仅仅是一个例子，还有很多其他例子。如果这种趋势继续发展下去，就会因为缺乏对大自然的尊重和这些地方大量的人类涉足，导致今后将没有其他地方的自然美景留给人们欣赏。

总之，因为发展中国家在"追赶"过程中所表现的急切和拼命，它们正在摧毁那些最初让自身独一无二的美景。这不仅是一种消极的发展态势，也是一种自我毁灭的发展态势。

Example 2  *Approach*

▶ **Question Keywords 题目关键词**

more countries developing tourism – why?

positive or negative?

▶ **Ideas 构思**

poorer countries can grow economy = destroy natural places

TV can make places popular → the beach in Thailand

| Examiner's Comment | | | |
|---|---|---|---|
| Coherence and Cohesion | Logical | ☑ | |
| | Progression | This is merely one, there are many others, If..., In conclusion | ☑ |
| Lexical Resource | Range | short, medium; negative, self-destructive | ☑ |
| | Less Common | catastrophic, aspect, outweighs, sheer | ☑ |
| Grammatical Range and Accuracy | Simple Structures | ☑ | |
| | Complex Structures | ☑ | |

**Example 3**  *Question and Answer*

*You should spend about 40 minutes on this task.*

*Write about the following topic:*

> **Across the world today, only a few languages are increasing in use, while the use of many other languages is declining.**
>
> **Is this a positive or negative development?**

*Give reasons for your answer and include any relevant examples from your own knowledge or experience.*

*Write at least 250 words.*

The following essay will explain why I believe that the fact that some languages are growing in use whereas 'many' others are fading away is a good thing.

To begin with, I believe communication is vital in today's world. Globalisation, the Internet and convenient international travel have brought us closer together, but that does not necessarily mean we can talk to each other. For many years, English has been the de facto standard language in most business dealings, even if it is not the first language of many countries. Also, with China still developing at phenomenal rates, more and more of the world's population is learning Chinese to do business here. Although there is a multitude of languages/dialects throughout China, the one that everyone speaks is known as Mandarin, the common speech.

Although I can understand why some people want to hold on to their language: they believe it is part of their roots, I think people should look forward rather than backward. The people of Wales have had a recent boost in people learning their language because of a learning app, but when very few people outside Wales can understand them, I fail to see the benefit of maintaining it.

In conclusion, I firmly believe that if the world can have only a few languages that everyone can understand, and when I say a few, I'm envisaging two or maybe three: Chinese, English and Spanish as an idea I think that not only will it bring us closer together in a business and economic sense, but also together as people as we will understand each other without the need for translators and potential misunderstandings.

**Word Count: 275**

下面的文章将解释为何我认为一些语言正在日益增加使用，而"许多"其他语言正在消失是一件好事。

首先，我认为沟通在当今世界至关重要。全球化、互联网和便捷的国际旅游让我们更密切联系，但这并不一定意味着我们可以彼此交谈。多年来，尽管英语不是许多国家的第一语言，却始终是大多数商业交易中实际存在的标准语言。此外，随着中国仍在以惊人的速度发展，越来越多的世界人口正在学习中文，以便在该国经商。尽管中国有多种语言或方言，但所有人都说着一种通用语言，即普通话。

虽然我能理解为何有些人想要坚持用自己的语言——他们认为这是他们文化根源的一部分，我认为人应该向前看而不是向后看。因为一个学习APP的出现，威尔士人近期在学习他们的语言方面有了很大的提高，但威尔士以外的人却很少能理解他们，所以我看不出保留这种语言的好处。

总之，我坚信，如果世界上只有几种人人都能理解的语言，而且我说的几种是指两种或三种：汉语、英语和西班牙语，作为一种理念，我认为这不仅会在商业和经济意义上让我们更密切联系，而且会让我们以人类的身份更密切联系，其原因是我们将相互理解，而不需要翻译，也没有潜在的误解。

## Example 3 *Approach*

### ▶ Question Keywords 题目关键词

world, few languages increasing, many languages declining

positive or negative?

### ▶ Ideas 构思

globalisation → English for business

roots, traditions → learning apps

| Examiner's Comment | | | |
|---|---|---|---|
| Coherence and Cohesion | Logical | ☑ | |
| | Progression | To begin with, Although, In conclusion | ☑ |
| Lexical Resource | Range | languages, dialects | ☑ |
| | Less Common | Globalisation, de facto, phenomenal, potential | ☑ |
| Grammatical Range and Accuracy | Simple Structures | ☑ | |
| | Complex Structures | ☑ | |

Example 4　*Question and Answer*

*You should spend about 40 minutes on this task.*

*Write about the following topic:*

> **People are buying more and more manufactured products to use or own.**
>
> **What effects do this have on the individual and on society?**
>
> **Is this a positive or negative development?**

*Give reasons for your answer and include any relevant examples from your own knowledge or experience.*

*Write at least 250 words.*

The statement given states that people are buying more manufactured goods to keep as their belongings, but what effect does this have on society, and is this a positive or negative development? In this essay, I will mention why I believe it to be a positive development.

This is a good question because I firmly believe that buying manufactured items is essential to our daily lives and helps to boost our local economies. Also, shopping is not just about buying what we need, it is also a hobby for millions of people, and retail therapy can help us as individuals. Consumerism has developed a lot over recent years, making daily life easier. For example, we can purchase a wide range of items to make our home lives much more comfortable and enjoyable. While we become more dependent on these products, they can all help develop our society, especially electronic gadgets, which can enrich our daily communication experiences.

On the other hand, it is fair to say that many unnecessary products on the market serve little purpose to most people. Still, most of the things we buy are of practical use, leading to a more positive and developed society. Also, there are often new and innovative products which, for me, I love to buy as they often use cutting-edge technology and, to be honest, I see them as being a fashion accessory too, which gives me more confidence as a person.

So, all in all, I feel good when I have new products and in my opinion, and I am sure many other people feel the same, this is a positive development for individuals and our society as a whole.

**Word Count: 279**

题目指出，人们不断购买更多的制成品作为其财产，但这对社会有什么影响？这是积极还是消极的发展态势？在这篇文章中，我将提到为何我认为这是一种积极的发展态势。

这是一个很好的问题，因为我坚信购买制成品对我们的日常生活至关重要，而且还有助于促进我们当地的经济。此外，购物不仅仅是购买我们需要的商品，还是数百万人的爱好，而购物疗法也可以帮助我们个人。消费主义近年来飞速发展，由此让日常生活变得更容易些。例如，我们可以购买各种各样的商品，让我们的家居生活更加舒适和愉快。虽然我们变得越来越依赖这些产品，但它们都有助于发展我们的社会，尤其是电子产品，它们可以丰富我们的日常通信体验。

另一方面，恰当地说，市场上许多不必要的产品对大多数人而言没有什么用处。尽管如此，我们购买的大部分商品都具有实际用途，可以让社会变得更加积极和发达。此外，对我而言，市面上经常会有新产品和创新产品，我喜欢购买这些产品，因为它们经常采用尖端技术，说实话，我也将其视为时尚配饰，这为我增添了更多自信。

因此，总体而言，在我购得新产品时，我感觉很好。在我看来，我确信许多其他人也有同感，这对个人和我们整个社会都是一种积极的发展态势。

## Example 4 *Approach*

### ▶ Question Keywords 题目关键词

buying more products

effects on individual and society

positive or negative?

### ▶ Ideas 构思

manufactured products = good → shopping = enjoyable

most products necessary = innovation = good for society

| Examiner's Comment | | | |
|---|---|---|---|
| Coherence and Cohesion | Logical | ☑ | |
| | Progression | Also, On the other hand, So, all in all | ☑ |
| Lexical Resource | Range | shopping, retail therapy; unnecessary, practical | ☑ |
| | Less Common | essential, gadgets, enrich, cutting-edge, fashion | ☑ |
| Grammatical Range and Accuracy | Simple Structures | ☑ | |
| | Complex Structures | ☑ | |

Example 5    *Question and Answer*

*You should spend about 40 minutes on this task.*

*Write about the following topic:*

> **Around the world it is likely that more adults will work from home, and more children will study from home, as computer technology becomes cheaper and more accessible.**
>
> **Do you think this will be a positive or negative development?**

*Give reasons for your answer and include any relevant examples from your own knowledge or experience.*

*Write at least 250 words.*

The statement poses whether the idea of adults working from home and children studying at home due to technology being more widely available is a good or bad development. The following essay will describe why I believe it would be a poor state of affairs if this were to happen.

Firstly, with the recent pandemic that occurred around the world, one thing that nearly everyone can agree on is that we need 'to get out of the house'. They have been constant reports over the last few years saying that parents do not know what to do with their children if they do not or can not go to school. So if the trend is set that more adults are expected to work online, and children study on their computers, I personally think that it would be a social disaster.

Secondly, there are very few jobs that can actually be done effectively online. Many jobs in the primary or secondary sectors (agriculture and manufacturing) cannot realistically be performed without an actual person doing a real activity. It is only in tiny parts of the service industry where this is possible, and nearly all of them would be technologically based in the first place. I am suggesting areas like finance and IT would be fine, but this would again fall down concerning hospitals, restaurants and the like.

In conclusion, I think it would be a complete catastrophe if this trend were to become a reality for the reasons I have stated above, and I sincerely hope that it never does.

***Word Count: 259***

这个题目提出一个问题：由于技术的普及，成年人居家工作以及儿童在家学习的主意是好是坏。下面的文章将说明为何我认为如果发生这种情况，这将是一种糟糕的事态。

第一，随着近期世界各地发生的流行病，几乎每个人都认同的一件事就是，我们需要"走出家门"。在过去几年内，不断有报道称，如果孩子不去或无法上学，家长们都不知道拿自己的孩子怎么办。因此，如果趋势是更多的成年人在线上工作，而孩子们在电脑上学习，那我个人认为这将是一场社会灾难。

第二，线上实际能够有效完成的工作很少。如果没有实际人员从事实际活动，第一产业或第二产业（农业和制造业）的许多工作实际上就无法完成。只有服务行业中极小的部分才可行，而且几乎所有的服务行业首先都是以科技为基础。我认为像金融和信息技术这样的领域就还好，但涉及医院、餐馆等时，则会再次下降。

总之，我认为如果这种趋势因为我上面所说的原因而成为现实，那将是一场彻底的灾难，我真诚地希望它永远不会发生。

## Example 5  *Approach*

### ▶ Question Keywords 题目关键词

more adults work and more children study from home because computer technology cheaper positive or negative?

### ▶ Ideas 构思

recent world pandemic = more people at home = bad for social skills

few online jobs = hospitals, restaurants

| Examiner's Comment | | | |
|---|---|---|---|
| Coherence and Cohesion | Logical | √ | |
| | Progression | Firstly, So, Secondly, In conclusion | √ |
| Lexical Resource | Range | bad, poor state | √ |
| | Less Common | constant, realistically, catastrophe, sincerely | √ |
| Grammatical Range and Accuracy | Simple Structures | √ | |
| | Complex Structures | √ | |

Example 6  *Question and Answer*

*You should spend about 40 minutes on this task.*

*Write about the following topic:*

> **Fossil fuels (e.g. coal, oil and natural gas) are the main source of energy in many countries. However, in some countries the use of alternative sources of energy (e.g. wind power and solar power) is encouraged.**
>
> **Is this a positive or negative development?**

*Give reasons for your answer and include any relevant examples from your own knowledge or experience.*

*Write at least 250 words.*

Fossil fuels continue to be the primary source of power and heating in many countries around the world. Recently, however, governments have been pushing for renewable options. Personally, I believe that this is a hugely positive move and should be encouraged further.

To begin with, it is well known that the emissions from fossil fuel power stations over the years have damaged the environment considerably and continue to do so. Unless this unrelenting degradation is halted and even reversed, we have a very bleak future on this planet. I believe that some governments have now made progress politically in promoting more environmentally friendly power sources, such as wind or solar, which is a significant step in the right direction. I sincerely hope the *Paris Accord* can meet everyone's expectations.

Technologically, as well as the ability to sustain supply, make sense to look for, and create, renewable energy sources. Fossil fuels, such as coal and oil, only have a finite amount left available, and we will reach, sooner rather than later, in my view, their limit. Therefore the newly created wind and solar farms in China that now create up to 11% of their gross energy use are truly visionary.

In conclusion then, as I have outlined above, I firmly believe that governments and countries that are encouraging the use of renewable, environmentally friendly energy generation are definitely doing the right thing and should be further implemented for the sake of future generations and the continuation of life on our little blue marble.

**Word Count: 252**

在世界许多国家，化石燃料仍然是电力和供暖的主要来源。然而，近期政府一直在推动可再生能源备选方案。我个人认为，这是一项非常积极的举措，应该进一步鼓励。

首先，众所周知，多年来化石燃料发电站的排放物对环境造成了相当大的破坏，而且这种破坏还在继续。除非停止甚至扭转这种持续恶化的局面，否则我们所生活的地球的未来将非常黯淡。我认为，一些政府目前在推广更环保的能源（如风能或太阳能）方面已经取得政治进展，这是朝着正确方向迈出的重要一步。我真诚地希望《巴黎协定》能够满足所有人的期望。

从技术以及维持供应的能力而言，寻找和创造可再生能源很有意义。煤和石油等化石燃料的可用量有限，在我看来，我们将很快达到化石燃料的可用量极限。因此，中国新建的风能和太阳能发电厂目前创造了高达 11% 的总能源使用量，这是真正的远见。

最后，正如我在上文所概述的那样，我坚信鼓励使用可再生、环保能源的政府和国家肯定是在做正确的事情，为了子孙后代，为了我们地球这个蓝色小星球上生命的延续，应该进一步实施这些措施。

## Example 6 *Approach*

### ▶ Question Keywords 题目关键词

many countries = fossil fuels main source of energy

other countries = more wind power and solar power

positive or negative?

### ▶ Ideas 构思

fossil emissions damaged environment → now changing

finite amount of fossil fuels = need for other forms

| | Examiner's Comment | | |
|---|---|---|---|
| Coherence and Cohesion | Logical | ☑ | |
| | Progression | To begin with, In conclusion | ☑ |
| Lexical Resource | Range | renewable, environmentally friendly, wind, solar | ☑ |
| | Less Common | renewable, unrelenting degradation, bleak, visionary | ☑ |
| Grammatical Range and Accuracy | Simple Structures | ☑ | |
| | Complex Structures | ☑ | |

Example 7    *Question and Answer*

*You should spend about 40 minutes on this task.*

*Write about the following topic:*

> **Some students take a year off between finishing school and going to university in order to travel or to work.**
>
> **Do the advantages outweigh the disadvantages?**

*Give reasons for your answer and include any relevant examples from your own knowledge or experience.*

*Write at least 250 words.*

For many students around the world, taking a gap year before starting university is a common practice, especially in Western countries. Although there are advantages to this, I believe that these days, they do not outweigh the disadvantages.

To begin with, these days a high-level education is becoming more and more necessary for future career prospects, not to mention that places are more competitive. This means that people will need to study for longer: into their mid or even late twenties. Therefore, adding another year to this at the beginning, I believe, is a waste of time as any work experience gained may be out of date, and if the year is just for travel, they would be at a disadvantage as they would be older than other job applicants.

On top of that, in my humble opinion, work experience is less necessary these days because companies expect to give new recruits full training when they begin work. They often give fast-track management programmes to graduates, and the higher your qualification, the higher you are likely to go in the company. This would definitely be the case for any scientific major where the aim is to become a researcher, or even a teacher.

In conclusion, although previously it may have been advantageous to broaden your horizons and potentially learn about different cultures, or gain some simple work experience, I think that the learning attitude has changed and that it is become more critical to obtain a higher education level and only then begin work.

***Word Count: 253***

对于世界各地许多学生而言，尤其是在西方国家，开始上大学之前的间休年是一种常见的做法。虽然这样做有好处，但我认为如今间休年弊大于利。

首先，如今未来职业前景变得越来越迫切需要高等教育，更不用说职位竞争更为激烈。这意味着人们将需要学习更长的时间，直到25岁左右甚至近30岁。因此，我认为，在开始上大学时再增加一年是在浪费时间，因为所获得的任何工作经验都有可能过时，如果这一年只是为了旅行，那他们将处于不利地位，因为他们的年龄会比其他求职者大。

依我拙见，最重要的是如今工作经验没那么必要，因为公司希望在新员工开始工作时为其提供充分的培训。这些公司经常会为毕业生提供快速管理课程，你的资历越高，在公司的职位就越高。对于任何以成为一名研究人员甚至是一名教师为目标的科学专业而言，情况更是如此。

总之，虽然先前间休年可能有利于拓宽你的视野，潜在地了解不同的文化，或者获得一些简单的工作经验，但我认为学习态度已经发生变化，获得高等教育之后才开始工作变得更加重要。

## Example 7　*Approach*

### ❯ Question Keywords 题目关键词

students, year off before university, travel or work

advantages more than disadvantages?

### ❯ Ideas 构思

disadvantages more

students study longer now – need Master's and PhD

experience less necessary

| Examiner's Comment | | | |
|---|---|---|---|
| Coherence and Cohesion | Logical | ☑ | |
| | Progression | To begin with, On top of that, In conclusion | ☑ |
| Lexical Resource | Range | education, management programmes, learning | ☑ |
| | Less Common | humble, fast-track, critical, obtain | ☑ |
| Grammatical Range and Accuracy | Simple Structures | ☑ | |
| | Complex Structures | ☑ | |

# Other Question Types

Example 1 *Question and Answer*

*You should spend about 40 minutes on this task.*

*Write about the following topic:*

> **In many cities, the quality of life is becoming worse.**
>
> **What do you think are the causes of this problem?**
>
> **What measures could be taken to solve it?**

*Give reasons for your answer and include any relevant examples from your own knowledge or experience.*

*Write at least 250 words.*

Large cities in various countries are not offering the quality of life they once did. The following essay will describe why I think this is happening and what can be done about it.

I think one of the leading causes of this problem is simply that there are simply too many people trying to live in them. With the constant influx of people who need infrastructure, housing, schools, electricity, parks and the like, it is incredibly difficult to supply these in an ever-growing city, and certainly at the required speed. Take New York as an example. Hundreds of thousands of people go there each year looking for work, education or a better life. They find comparatively expensive food and accommodation, traffic jams and ever-increasing scores to attend university.

In order to alleviate this issue, I personally believe that the government needs to focus on creating jobs and infrastructure in the more rural areas so that there is no need for the people living in those areas to move towards, or even into, the cities. Taking the US as an example, the migration into large cities like New York, Los Angeles or even Chicago and Boston has made their environments, in my view, unsustainable. I do not believe the current growth rate can continue into the mid or long-term future. Therefore, developing areas around these cities would be a good idea.

In conclusion, the qualities that those moving to the big cities seek are being diminished. Only the government can reduce this ever-growing problem through direct intervention and investment.

***Word Count: 258***

许多国家的大城市不再像以前那样提供高品质的生活。下面的文章将说明为何我认为会发生这种情况以及可以采取何种应对措施。

我认为这个问题的一个主要原因是有太多的人试图居住在城市。随着需要基础设施、住房、学校、电力、公园等设施的人员不断涌入，在一个不断发展的城市中以所需速度提供这些设施相当困难。以纽约为例。每年有成千上万的人员前往纽约寻找工作、教育或更好的生活。他们发现纽约食宿费用相对昂贵，交通拥挤且大学录取分数不断增加。

为了缓解这一问题，我个人认为，政府需要把重点放在在更多的农村地区创造就业机会和建设基础设施之上，由此生活在农村地区的人员就没有必要向城市迁移，甚至进入城市。以美国为例，在我看来，向纽约、洛杉矶甚至芝加哥和波士顿这样的大城市迁移会让这些城市的环境变得不可持续发展。我认为当前的经济增长率不会持续到中长期。因此，在这些城市周围开发片区会是一个不错的主意。

总之，那些迁移到大城市的人员所追求的品质正在不断降低。只有政府才能通过直接干预和投资来缓解这个日益严重的问题。

### Example 1   *Approach*

▶ **Question Keywords 题目关键词**

many cities, quality of life worse

causes?

how to solve it

▶ **Ideas 构思**

too many people moving to them → New York

job creation, infrastructure in rural/surrounding areas

| Examiner's Comment | | | |
|---|---|---|---|
| Coherence and Cohesion | Logical | ☑ | |
| | Progression | the leading causes, In order to, In conclusion | ☑ |
| Lexical Resource | Range | ☑ | |
| | Less Common | influx, infrastructure, focus, unsustainable | ☑ |
| Grammatical Range and Accuracy | Simple Structures | ☑ | |
| | Complex Structures | ☑ | |

**Example 2** *Question and Answer*

*You should spend about 40 minutes on this task.*

*Write about the following topic:*

> **Nowadays many charities and other organisations publicise their activities by giving a name to a particular day every day. These include 'Children's Day', to encourage better treatment of children, and 'Non-Smoking Day', to encourage people to give up smoking.**
>
> **Why do you think organisations are introducing these special days?**
>
> **How effective can these days be?**

*Give reasons for your answer and include any relevant examples from your own knowledge or experience.*

*Write at least 250 words.*

These days there are a number of different companies, charities, and the like are bringing in their own unique 'days'. The examples given are 'Children's Day' and 'Non-Smoking Day'. The following essay will explain why I believe these entities are creating these anomalous days and whether or not they can be effective in today's society.

To begin with, I believe the main reason that organisations create these days is marketing. Whether this be the Red Cross, Children in Need from the charity side of things, or Alibaba and JD, from the commercial side, I believe that the purpose is the same: to highlight the organisation's activities and raise money. This can be shown either as enormous profits for a company or increased awareness for a charity cause.

The increased popularity and the rising number of 'special days' show us that the idea is good and that more and more organisations are jumping on the bandwagon. I have seen news reports showing 'record sales' for Alibaba year on year since 'singles' day' emerged. I am unfamiliar with the exact number of people that have stopped smoking because of the Non-Smoking Day, but I would assume it is also popular and rising, mainly because it is still happening.

In conclusion, I believe these days are being introduced more and more, which shows the concept's effectiveness. It is now a worldwide phenomenon with a more significant number of global organisations developing their own 'days'. In my opinion, this trend is only set to continue and grow.

***Word Count: 253***

如今，有许多不同的公司、慈善机构等都推出了自己独特的"节日"。例如"儿童节"和"无烟日"。下面的文章将解释为何我认为这些实体是在设立这些非传统意义上的节日，及其在当今社会是否有效。

首先，我认为组织机构设立这些节日的主要原因是营销。无论是从慈善角度考虑的红十字会和儿童救助组织，还是从商业角度考虑的阿里巴巴和京东，我认为其设立节日的目的都一样——突出组织机构活动并筹集资金。这既可以表现为公司的巨额利润，也可以表现为慈善事业知名度的提升。

越来越受欢迎和越来越多的"特殊节日"向我们表明，这个主意不错，而且越来越多的组织机构也加入这一行列。我看到新闻报道显示，自"光棍节"推出以来，阿里巴巴年年"销售额创新高"。我不清楚因为"无烟日"而停止吸烟的确切人数，但我认为这个节日也很受欢迎，而且不断上升，原因主要是其仍在发生。

总之，我认为这些节日的引入正在不断增加，这表明这一概念的有效性。随着越来越多的全球性组织机构开始设立自身的"节日"，现在这已经成为一种全球现象。在我看来，这种趋势只会继续发展。

## Example 2  *Approach*

▶ **Question Keywords** 题目关键词

charities, publicise, give a name to a day, e.g. Children's Day

why do companies do this?

are they effective?

▶ **Ideas** 构思

marketing – example → Red Cross, Children in Need, Alibaba, JD

yes → record sales for companies

now well known → singles' day

| Examiner's Comment | | | |
|---|---|---|---|
| Coherence and Cohesion | Logical | ☑ | |
| | Progression | To begin with, In conclusion | ☑ |
| Lexical Resource | Range | organisations, commercial | ☑ |
| | Less Common | bandwagon, concept, phenomenon | ☑ |
| Grammatical Range and Accuracy | Simple Structures | ☑ | |
| | Complex Structures | ☑ | |

Example 3    *Question and Answer*

*You should spend about 40 minutes on this task.*

*Write about the following topic:*

> **Studies suggest children now watch much more television than they did in the past and spend less time doing active or creative things.**
>
> **Why do you think this is the case?**
>
> **What measures could be taken to encourage children to spend more time doing active and creative things?**

*Give reasons for your answer and include any relevant examples from your own knowledge or experience.*

*Write at least 250 words.*

Apparently, children these days watch more TV now and spend less time being active or creative than their predecessors. The following essay will describe why I think this is so and how we can change this habit.

To begin with, the why. I believe that the fact that TV is more available now is the most prominent and straightforward answer. Here in India, for example, 40 or 50 years ago, many families did not even own a TV and everyone, including my parents, would go to the one house in the village where they had one and spend a few hours watching the latest shows. The rest of the time, it simply wasn't available. These days, you can not get away from it. iQIYI, TikTok, NetFlix, Amazon and many other companies stream to computers, tablets and phones in a constant barrage of entertainment. There is no wonder that children pick up on it and that it has now become the 'third' parent.

There are many actions that, in my opinion, could be taken to change this situation. Most importantly, the parents, or grandparents, simply need to spend more time with the children and not just give them a smartphone to play with to shut them up. It takes time and effort, but if these are spent, the child will get used to being more active. As for the creative side, I believe that it really is up to the individual. Many youngsters are not creative, myself included, but a very small child will still enjoy getting dirty with paint and some paper over a colour the lines app.

Overall, I think it is up to the parents and guardians to instigate new ideas to spend time with their kids so that they are well-rounded and do not fall back on the crutch of multimedia simply because it is easy.

***Word Count: 308***

显然，现在的孩子比他们的前辈收看更多的电视，花费更少的时间来保持积极主动状态或创造力。下面的文章将说明为何我认为情况如此，以及我们如何改变这种习惯。

首先，说明原因。我认为，现在电视更加普及是最突出和直接的答案。例如，在印度，四五十年前，许多家庭甚至没有电视，包括我父母在内的每个人都会跑去村里有电视的人家里花费几个小时收看最新电视节目。而他们在其余时间根本没办法收看电视节目。如今却随处可见。爱奇艺、抖音、网飞、亚马逊和许多其他公司源源不断地向电脑、平板电脑和手机播放娱乐节目。难怪孩子会喜欢收看电视、网络等媒体上的节目，而且这现在已经成为"第三"父母。

在我看来，可以采取许多措施来改变这种状况。最重要的是，父母或祖父母需要做的只是花费更多的时间陪伴孩子，而不只是给他们一部智能手机让他们玩耍，让他们安静。这需要时间和精力，但如果同时花费了时间和精力，孩子将会习惯于变得更加积极主动。至于创造性方面，我认为这确实取决于个人。包括我自己在内的许多年轻人没有创造力，但一个年幼的小孩仍喜欢在线条涂色应用软件上通过颜料和一些画纸而弄脏自己。

总体而言，我认为这取决于父母和监护人激发出花费时间和他们的孩子待在一起的新想法，这样他们才可得到全面发展，而不是仅仅因为简单而借助多媒体的帮助。

## Example 3 *Approach*

### ▶ Question Keywords 题目关键词

children watch more TV than the past, spend less time doing active or creative things

why?

how to encourage children to do active or creative things

### ▶ Ideas 构思

TV more available, more streaming services → TikTok, iQIYI, etc.

spend time with family, encourage creativity → painting

| Examiner's Comment | | | |
|---|---|---|---|
| Coherence and Cohesion | Logical | ☑ | |
| | Progression | To begin with, As for the, Overall | ☑ |
| Lexical Resource | Range | children, youngsters, kids | ☑ |
| | Less Common | prominent, well-rounded, crutch | ☑ |
| Grammatical Range and Accuracy | Simple Structures | ☑ | |
| | Complex Structures | ☑ | |

**Example 4** *Question and Answer*

*You should spend about 40 minutes on this task.*

*Write about the following topic:*

> **Some ex-prisoners commit crimes after being released from the prison.**
>
> **What do you think is the cause?**
>
> **How can it be solved?**

*Give reasons for your answer and include any relevant examples from your own knowledge or experience.*

*Write at least 250 words.*

Repeat offenders in the criminal justice system are a fact of life, but we as a society must try and understand why this happens and whether anything can be done to solve, or at least reduce, the number.

If we first look at the reasons why convicts re-offend soon after leaving prison. In order to do that, I believe we should first look at why they were in prison in the first place, and for what kind of crime they were imprisoned. If, for example, the person has not finished, or even did not go to school, and was caught stealing food or clothing, it could be that the person involved believes he had no other choice. He/She was simply trying to survive. If, however, the person committed some form of violent crime like manslaughter or murder, again this needs to be looked at closely as it could have been pre-meditated, or simply an accident. Either way, with the examples shown above, by purely locking these people up, there is no rehabilitation process and no foreseeable future after their release.

One potential solution to this problem could be academic or vocational education. For the thief that did not finish high school, he could, while incarcerated, finish his diploma. Depending on the length of his sentence, maybe even do a degree. When released, he will have a much better opportunity to find a job. For the person who killed someone, let say by vehicular manslaughter, he could be further educated in driving skills and taught, if he did not already realise, the consequences of driving whilst drunk.

In conclusion, I genuinely believe that education can greatly benefit some offenders so that they have more opportunities when leaving prison, which in turn means that they will not re-offend.

***Word Count: 296***

刑事司法系统中的惯犯是现实，但作为一个社会，我们必须尝试和理解为什么会发生这种情况，以及是否可采取任何应对措施来解决或至少减少该数字。

如果我们先看罪犯出狱后不久再次犯罪的原因。为了做到这一点，我认为我们首先应看看他们入狱的原因，以及他们因何种类型的罪行而被监禁。例如，如果此人尚未完成学业，或甚至没有上学，且在偷食物或衣服时被逮捕，这或许是因为涉事人员认为自己别无选择。他（她）只是想活下去。然而，如果此人犯了某种形式的暴力罪行，例如过失杀人或谋杀，这同样需要仔细审查，因为这种罪行可能是预谋划，或者只是一个意外。无论属于哪种方式，通过上面列举的例子，仅仅将这些人关进监狱，会让他们在获释后没有改过自新的过程，也没有可预见的未来。

该问题的一个潜在解决方案可能是学术或职业教育。对于未完成高中学业的小偷而言，他可以在监禁期间完成他的文凭课程。根据其刑期的长短，甚至可能获得学位。在获释后，他将有更好的机会找到工作。对于杀人犯（如因车辆过失导致人亡）而言，如果他未意识到酒后驾驶的后果，则他可接受进一步的驾驶技能教育和授课。

总之，我真诚地认为，教育可使一些罪犯受益良多，让他们出狱时拥有更多的机会，这反过来意味着他们不会再次犯罪。

## Example 4 *Approach*

▶ **Question Keywords** 题目关键词

ex-prisoners commit crimes again, after prison

why?

solution?

▶ **Ideas** 构思

don't know anything else, uneducated, can't find a job

education and training

| Examiner's Comment | | | |
|---|---|---|---|
| Coherence and Cohesion | Logical | ☑ | |
| | Progression | If we first look at, In conclusion | ☑ |
| Lexical Resource | Range | Repeat offenders, re-offend | ☑ |
| | Less Common | imprisoned, manslaughter, pre-meditated | ☑ |
| Grammatical Range and Accuracy | Simple Structures | ☑ | |
| | Complex Structures | ☑ | |

Important Point: *This again is a very similar question to Example 2 in 'To what extent do you agree or disagree?' I've deliberately used the ideas given in that question to show you an opposing idea of the previous example answer.*

**重点**：这也是一个与 To what extent do you agree or disagree? 的 Example 2 非常相似的问题。我有意用那个问题给出的观点向你们展示了与前面例文相反的观点。

**Example 5** *Question and Answer*

*You should spend about 40 minutes on this task.*

*Write about the following topic:*

> **Young people do not spend their holiday and weekend doing outdoor activities like hiking and climbing in natural environment.**
>
> **Why?**
>
> **How to encourage them to go out?**

*Give reasons for your answer and include any relevant examples from your own knowledge or experience.*

*Write at least 250 words.*

It is been suggested that the younger generation spend most of their holidays and weekends indoors rather than doing outdoor activities like hiking along trails or climbing mountains. In the essay, I will look into the possible reasons for this as well as some ideas on how to 'get them out of the house'.

To look at the 'Why?' question first, I think we need to look at the availability of other things to do besides going outside. The first ones that come to mind are TV and video games. Two, or even one generation ago, these were not readily available in all households. Therefore, the desire to stay inside was not as great as it is today. TV and game consoles can be very compelling to kids, as an avid gamer myself, I can confirm this, and as they all need electricity to work, confine them to the inside world of the lounge or bedroom rather than the outside world of the garden or field.

Moving onto ideas on how to get these couch potatoes outside, is more difficult to answer. I believe that the primary solution would be for parents to spend more time with the children. Many parents think that the TV is a good nanny and keeps their children safe and out of mischief. What they do not always realise is that the habit is difficult to break and that children get more attention from the TV than mum and dad. If the family as a whole gets into the habit of spending time outside together, I believe it is more likely that the children will go out even if the parents are busy.

In conclusion, I believe it is all about the habits children get into when they are very young that make all the difference to their behaviours later.

***Word Count: 305***

有人认为，年轻一代将其大部分假期和周末时间花费在室内，而不是进行室外活动，例如沿着小路徒步或爬山。在本文中，我将探索这种情况的可能原因，以及关于如何"使他们走出家门"的一些想法。

　　先看"为什么？"这个问题。我认为我们需要看看除了外出之外是否还有其他事情可以做。首先会想到的是电视和电子游戏。在两代人甚至一代人以前，并不是所有家庭都能轻易获得电视和电子游戏。因此，待在室内的愿望并不像今天这样强烈。电视和游戏机对孩子们来说非常有吸引力，本人作为一名狂热的游戏玩家，可以证实这一点，而且因为电视和游戏机都需要用电，使他们被限制在内部世界的客厅或卧室，而不是外部世界的花园或田野。

　　说到如何让这些整天看电视的人走出去，这更难回答。我认为主要的解决办法是父母花更多的时间和孩子待在一起。许多父母认为电视是一个好保姆，可以保护孩子安全，也不搞恶作剧。他们始终没意识到的是，这个习惯很难打破，而且孩子们从电视上获得的关注比父母更多。如果整个家庭养成了花时间共同到室外活动的习惯，那么我相信即使父母很忙，孩子们也更有可能到室外活动。

　　总之，我相信孩子们在很小的时候养成的习惯会对他们以后的行为产生很大影响。

## Example 5　*Approach*

▶ **Question Keywords 题目关键词**

young people, don't go out on holidays or weekends, outdoor activities = hiking and climbing

why?

how to encourage them to do so?

▶ **Ideas 构思**

why – TV, video games, smartphone games

solution = early habits, get the family out together

| Examiner's Comment | | | |
|---|---|---|---|
| Coherence and Cohesion | Logical | ☑ | |
| | Progression | To look at…first, Moving onto, In conclusion | ☑ |
| Lexical Resource | Range | video games, consoles; kids, children | ☑ |
| | Less Common | desire, compelling, confine, couch potatoes, mischief | ☑ |
| Grammatical Range and Accuracy | Simple Structures | ☑ | |
| | Complex Structures | ☑ | |

| Example 6 | *Question and Answer* |

*You should spend about 40 minutes on this task.*

*Write about the following topic:*

> **The level of noise around us is constantly increasing and is affecting the quality of our lives.**
>
> **What causes the noise?**
>
> **What should be done about it?**

*Give reasons for your answer and include any relevant examples from your own knowledge or experience.*

*Write at least 250 words.*

We now live in a time where there is constant background noise, and this seems not only to be growing in quantity, but also in volume. I will define what I believe to be the major causes of this and also what can be done to make the world a slightly quieter place.

You can take your pick these days at what noise affects you the most. It could be traffic, trains, mobile ringtones, outdoor music, or just people talking. Some of these will depend on where you live, but for me, I will encounter some or all of these on an average day to varying degrees. It is an inescapable, and highly annoying, part of everyday life.

Solving this problem is a lot more difficult than it first appears. It would be impossible to eliminate all noise from a rural area, let alone an urban one. I do think it could be improved by introducing 'quiet zones' into some areas. For example, having one carriage on a train where you cannot use a mobile phone is something that I have seen in Europe. Not being able to use your car horn in some residential areas, would be another possible solution that already exists in some cities here in China.

In conclusion, I believe that there should be areas where people can find peace in whatever noise is being created. This will have to be thought about creatively, as it may be difficult to do effectively. If it can be successfully completed though, I am sure everyone will be much happier.

***Word Count: 261***

我们现在生活在一个持续有背景噪音的时代，而且这种噪音似乎不仅在数量上增长，在音量上也有所提高。我将解释我认为造成这种情况的主要原因，以及可以做些什么来使世界变得稍微安静一点。

现在你可以任意选择哪些噪音对你的影响最大。可能是车流声、火车声、手机铃声、室外音乐，或只是人们的谈话声。其中一些取决于你住在哪里，但对我而言，我每天都会遇到不同程度的其中一些或全部噪音。这种情况在日常生活中不可避免，也非常令人讨厌。

解决这个问题比最初看起来要困难得多。消除农村地区的所有噪音都不可能，更不用说城市了。我确实认为在一些区域中引入"安静区"可以改善这一情况。例如，我曾在欧洲见过在火车上有一节车厢不能使用手机。在一些居民区不能使用汽车喇叭，这可以是另一种可能的解决方案，在中国的一些城市也已经实施了。

总之，我认为应该有一些地方，不论产生了什么样的噪音，人们都能找到安静之处。这需要创造性地考虑，因为这可能很难有效地做到。如果能成功实现，我相信每个人都会更开心。

## Example 6 *Approach*

▶ **Question Keywords 题目关键词**

noise level increasing, affects quality of lives

what causes the noise?

do what?

▶ **Ideas 构思**

causes = transport, communication (smartphones)

do what = quiet zones

| | Examiner's Comment | | |
|---|---|---|---|
| Coherence and Cohesion | Logical | ☑ | |
| | Progression | define...the major causes, what can be done, In conclusion | ☑ |
| Lexical Resource | Range | quiet zones, cannot use a mobile phone, Not being able to use your car horn | ☑ |
| | Less Common | depend, varying degrees, residential | ☑ |
| Grammatical Range and Accuracy | Simple Structures | ☑ | |
| | Complex Structures | ☑ | |

Example 7    *Question and Answer*

*You should spend about 40 minutes on this task.*

*Write about the following topic:*

> **The natural resources such as oil, forests, and water are being consumed at an alarming rate.**
>
> **What problems does it cause?**
>
> **How can we solve these problems?**

*Give reasons for your answer and include any relevant examples from your own knowledge or experience.*

*Write at least 250 words.*

Our planet's resources are being used at an ever-increasing rate. The population around the world is growing, and the need for energy or water is increasing in line, causing many people a great deal of concern. Various problems can arise from this, including, but not limited to, the environmental impact as well as the simple truth that the resources are finite. Solutions are available and numerous, but rarely implemented to any effective level.

Beginning with the environmental issue, the mining and use of oil, deforestation, and water consumption for agricultural or other uses, all have different impacts on the environment. It is well known that the burning of oil creates greenhouse gases, one of the main issues around the current climate change crisis. Deforestation is linked to this, as fewer trees can absorb the $CO_2$ created by fossil fuel burning and mining. Water, is perhaps the largest resource on the planet, being two-thirds of its makeup. What is less understood however, is that only about 10% of that amount is useable as drinking water, or for agriculture. This all amounts to the fact that these are all finite resources and will run out at some point.

Solutions are possible to combat the problems I have identified, with the use of renewable energy resources being top of the list. China is leading the world in the creation of wind and solar energy farms so that we do not need to use oil for power stations and the like. It can simply be used for the other products it is used for, like plastics and the building trade. For the deforestation problem, I believe that we need to reduce the amount of trees being cut down to a level where the replacement of them is either greater, or at least the same level. Lastly, looking at the water, I believe we need a technological solution to either desalinate sea water, or recycle what we currently use more efficiently.

***Word Count: 325***

人类正以不断递增的速度使用我们的地球资源。世界人口正在不断增长，对能源和水的需求也在不断增长，这引起了许多人的极大关注。由此可能产生各种问题，包括但不限于对环境的影响，以及资源是有限的这一简单事实。解决方案是有的，也很多，但很少被实施到任何有效的程度。

先谈谈环境问题，石油的开采和使用、森林砍伐，以及农业或其他用途的用水，都对环境产生不同的影响。众所周知，燃烧石油会产生温室气体，这是当前气候变化危机的主要问题之一。森林砍伐与此相关，因为能够吸收化石燃料燃烧和采矿所产生的二氧化碳的树木更少了。水可能是地球上最大的资源，占地球构成的三分之二。然而，人们不太了解的是，其中只有大约10%可作为饮用水或农业用水。这一切都意味着，事实上这些都是有限的资源，总有一天会耗尽。

我所指出的这些问题是有可行的解决方案的，其中排在首位的是使用可再生能源。中国在风能和太阳能农场的建设方面处于世界领先地位，这样我们就不需要在发电站等设施上使用石油了。它可以只用于其他产品，比如塑料和建筑贸易。对于森林砍伐问题，我认为我们需要减少伐木数量，使它们的替换量更大，或至少减少到相同程度。最后，对于水资源，我认为我们需要一个技术解决方案来淡化海水，或更有效地回收我们目前使用的水。

## Example 7 *Approach*

▶ **Question Keywords 题目关键词**

resources = oil, forests, water – being consumed too quickly

problems?

solutions?

▶ **Ideas 构思**

problems = environmental, finite amount

solutions = renewable energy resources, recycling

| Examiner's Comment | | | |
|---|---|---|---|
| Coherence and Cohesion | Logical | ☑ | |
| | Progression | Beginning with, Lastly | ☑ |
| Lexical Resource | Range | ☑ | |
| | Less Common | implemented, deforestation, consumption, solar, desalinate | ☑ |
| Grammatical Range and Accuracy | Simple Structures | ☑ | |
| | Complex Structures | ☑ | |

Congratulations on finishing this part of the book! After going through these examples, I hope you better understand how to approach and structure your Task 2 essays.

恭喜你读完了本书这一部分！看过这些例子后，我希望你能更好地理解如何处理和组织你的 Task 2 文章。

As I mentioned in the Task 1 section summary, please don't just memorise these answers. You will need to analyse how I broke down each question so that you can properly understand what the question is asking and what ideas can be generated as an answer. Once this is done, it's just a case of getting those ideas down on paper in a logical order.

正如我在 Task 1 的小结中提到的，请不要仅仅背诵这些例文。你需要分析我是如何分解每个问题的，这样你才能正确理解这个题目在问什么，并产生作文构思。当这个步骤完成后，接下来就是把这些想法按照逻辑顺序写到试卷上了。

Don't forget, my suggestion is that you do this task first as it's worth more points than Task 1, and if you weren't to complete this task because you run out of time in the test, you'd lose more points.

别忘了，我的建议是你先写 Task 2，因为它的分值比 Task 1 高。而且，如果你因为时间关系不能完成 Task 2，那你会失分更多。

One more point to remember is that the examiner is not marking you for your opinion. They are marking for your ability to put your opinion on paper clearly, logically and correctly. As I mentioned earlier, none of the essays I have written necessarily show what I actually believe. They simply came into my mind first and what I found the easiest to write about.

还有一点要记住，考官不是根据你的观点给你打分。他们考查的是你清晰、有逻辑、正确地将自己的观点写在试卷上的能力。正如我之前提到的，我所写的例文中没有一篇必须表明我真正相信什么。这些想法只是出现在我的脑海里，而且我觉得最容易写。

An exercise you might like to try is to practise writing three essays for each question. One in agreement the situation, one against the situation and one where you are in the middle (neither agree nor disagree). This will give you some mental practise in looking at discussions and arguments from different sides.

你可能会想要试着做的练习是针对每个题目写三篇作文。一篇是你持支持观点的文章，一篇是你持反对意见的文章，另一篇是你持中立观点的文章。这样会帮助你从不同角度看待这些讨论与论点。

# Module Tests and Sample Answers

## 真题模拟及参考答案

### Task 1

*You should spend about 20 minutes on this task.*

**The chart below shows information about various professions in the U.K. and their salaries. The table shows the average working hours per week for each profession.**

**Summarise the information by selecting and reporting the main features, and make comparisons where relevant.**

*You should write at least 150 words.*

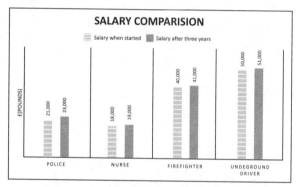

| Profession | Average working of hours per week |
|---|---|
| Police | 40 |
| Nurse | 38 |
| Firefighter | 55 |
| Underground Driver | 36 |

### Task 2

*You should spend about 40 minutes on this task.*

*Write about the following topic:*

**In some countries today, people are having their first child when they are older.**

**What are the reasons for this?**

**Do the advantages of this development outweigh the disadvantages?**

*Give reasons for your answer and include any relevant examples from your own knowledge or experience.*

*You should write at least 250 words.*

# Test 1 Sample Answers 试题 1 参考答案

The chart and table given show the starting salaries, income after 3 years and average working hours of four different public sector jobs: police, nursing, firefighting and tube driving.

Looking initially at the Salary comparison bar chart, it is clearer to see that Underground drivers have both the best starting salary and level after 3 years, 50k and 51k GBP. An increase of 1k GBP after three years which is fairly standard across the board with the exception of the Police force where it is 2k GBP. Firefighting in the second highest starting point, with 10k GBP less and the Police force with a further 19k GBP less. Nurses are at the bottom of the pile starting at just 18k GBP per year.

Moving onto the table, there is quite a difference between the hours. The highest amount is the Firefighters with 55, with Police and Nursing 15 to 17 hours less. The least is 36 hours by the underground workers.

In summary, perhaps surprisingly even though the tube drivers work the least hours and arguably have the least daily danger, they earn the most money.

***Word Count: 186***

所给图表显示了四种不同公共部门工作的起薪、三年后的收入和平均工作时间：分别是警察、护士、消防员和地铁驾驶员。

首先看一下薪资对比柱状图，可以更清晰地看到地铁驾驶员起薪和三年后的收入水平都是最高的，分别是5万英镑和5.1万英镑。三年后加薪1,000英镑，算是上述行业中的标准，除了加薪2,000英镑的警察部门。消防部门的起薪属于第二高，比第一高的收入少1万英镑，警察部门的起薪比消防部门又少了1.9万英镑。护士的起薪处于最底层，仅为每年1.8万英镑。

再来看一下表格，上述四种部门工作的平均工作时间之间存在很大差别。平均工作时间最长的是消防员（55小时），而警察和护士的平均工作时间比消防员分别少15和17个小时。平均工作时间最短的是地铁工作人员（36小时）。

总之，也许令人惊讶的是，尽管地铁驾驶员的平均工作时间最短，可以说每天面临的危险也最少，但他们赚的钱却最多。

In a few countries around the world, people are deciding to have children later in life. This essay will look at the why of this as well as whether this is a positive development.

Looking at the possible reasons for this new phenomenon, I believe we have to look at the changes in lifestyle and education. These days, male and female people are studying to a higher level, Master's or PhD, and then going to work. This means that they are much older when they graduate and begin relationships. Although it is possible that people meet and get together at university, the fact that they may change university between undergrad and postgrad courses means that they are more likely to meet their future wife or husband at work. I would be a classic example of this, as I will change university soon to progress to my Master's course.

Personally, I believe that this is a positive development. The fact that people are older means that they are more mature and should understand more about life, work, family and responsibility. Not only that, but the more educated a person is, the higher their salary will be when they are first hired and not in the future. Money is obviously an essential part of raising a family.

In conclusion, it is pretty apparent that the world is changing and that the younger generation believes in getting a firm base in education before looking to move down the family route. Because of the extra experience and life skills that this brings, I believe that they are more ready and prepared to have a family.

***Word Count: 271***

　　在世界上的一些国家中，人们正在决定晚育。这篇文章将研究这样做的原因，以及这样做是否是一个积极的发展态势。

　　考虑到这种新现象的可能原因，我认为我们必须看看生活方式和教育的变化。如今，男性和女性都在攻读更高学历，如硕士或者博士，之后才参加工作。这意味着当他们毕业并开始恋爱时，他们的年龄要大得多。尽管人们有可能在大学里认识并走到一起，但他们可能会在本科生和研究生课程之间更换大学，这意味着他们更有可能在工作中遇到未来的妻子或丈夫。我就是一个典型的例子，因为我很快会到另一所大学进修硕士课程。

　　我个人认为，这是一个积极的发展态势。事实上，人们年龄的增长意味着他们更加成熟，而且对生活、工作、家庭和责任的理解更深。不仅如此，一个人受教育程度越高，他们在第一次受雇时（而不是将来）的薪资越高。显然，钱是养家的基本部分。

　　总之，很明显世界正在发生变化，年轻一代认为在转战到家庭之前需要在教育方面打下坚实基础。因为他们拥有了更多经验和生活技能，我相信他们已经准备好组建家庭了。

Task 1

*You should spend about 20 minutes on this task.*

> The graph shows the number of people taking part in 4 kinds of sports in a particular region between 1985 and 2005.
>
> Summarise the information by selecting and reporting the main features, and make comparisons where relevant.

*You should write at least 150 words.*

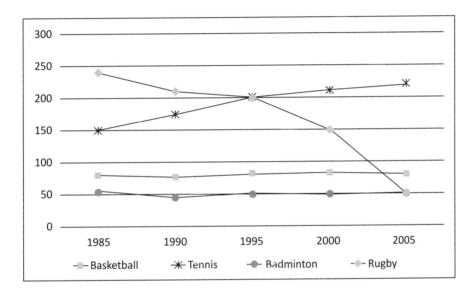

Task 2

*You should spend about 40 minutes on this task.*

*Write about the following topic:*

> More and more people are becoming seriously overweight. Some people suggest that the solution to this problem is to increase the price of fattening foods.
>
> To what extent do you agree or disagree?

*Give reasons for your answer and include any relevant examples from your own knowledge or experience.*

*You should write at least 250 words.*

### Task 1

The chart illustrates the quantity of people participating in 4 different kinds of sports, Basketball, Tennis, Badminton and Rugby, over a 20-year-period beginning in 1985. The statement does not indicate where the data is from, merely 'a particular region'.

Starting with the data of Basketball and Badminton. These are by far the least popular with Badminton hovering around the 50 mark throughout the entire 20 years and Basketball with not much more, maybe varying between 75-80.

Moving onto the second pair of sports, Tennis and Rugby. Tennis was the only sport with a significant increase. Starting at the 150 mark back in 1985, gently rising over two decades to finish at around the 225 point. Rugby had some disastrous figures starting a little less than 250 in 1985, matching the Tennis value in 1995 and dropping to 50, equal to Badminton, in 2005.

In summary then, the figures vary quite a lot from each other with both indoor sports remaining stable but the outdoor ones having opposite trends to each other.

***Word Count: 171***

> 　　这张图表显示了从1985年开始的20年间，参加篮球、网球、羽毛球和橄榄球这4种不同运动的人数。这份报告未指出数据来源，仅指出"某个特定地区"。
>
> 　　首先看篮球和羽毛球的数据。这两类运动是到目前为止受欢迎程度最低的，羽毛球在整个20年间一直只有大约50人参与，篮球也没有更多，可能在75-80人之间浮动。
>
> 　　再来看第二对运动：网球和橄榄球。网球是唯一参与人数有显著增长的运动。从1985年的150人开始，经过20年的缓慢上升，最终达到225人左右。橄榄球的数据非常不好，从1985年的略低于250人开始，到1995年与网球数据持平，然后到2005年降至50人，与羽毛球的参与人数相当。
>
> 　　总之，这些数据彼此之间相差很大，参加室内运动的人数均保持稳定，但参加室外运动的人数彼此之间呈相反趋势。

Obesity is a growing problem worldwide. People are getting heavier, which has the potential to cause a large number of health-related issues in the future. There have been a variety of solutions put forward over the years for this alarming trend, one of which is increasing the price of fattening foods. Although I do believe this is one of the more creative ideas, I do not believe it goes far enough on its own and will not be all that effective. I am going to look at this possible solution from two angles, firstly what the fattening foods actually are, and secondly, how much of an increase would be viable.

Fattening foods could be anything from Macdonald's Happy Meals, to ice cream, to Hula Hoops. It would first need to be decided what exactly fattening foods are and whether or not they would be considered a basic necessity. Take milk as an example. In countries like the US or UK, multiple types of milk are available, from skimmed to semi-skimmed to full fat. So the question then becomes, 'Should we increase the price of such a basic necessity, or should we concentrate on other products?' In my mind, this seems like a slippery slope because of how you would then categorise cheese and the like.

It has been previously shown with other price increases on specific food types, sugar to be specific, that unless there is a significant rise, and I am thinking doubling the price, or maybe even more, it will not have the desired effect and people may go without other foods in order to buy the fattening ones.

In conclusion, although raising the prices of fattening food is a good one, I believe it will be tricky to sort out which foods are too 'fattening' and how much the increase should be.

***Word Count: 305***

肥胖是一个全球范围内日益严重的问题。人们越来越胖，这有可能在未来引发大量与健康相关的问题。多年来，针对这一令人担忧的趋势，人们提出了各种解决方案，其中之一是提高致肥食品的价格。尽管我确实相信这是更有创意的想法之一，但我不相信单用这一个措施就足够，也不会那么有效。我将从两个角度来看这个可能的解决方案，第一，什么是真正的致肥食品，第二，致肥食品的价格提高多少才可行。

让人发胖的食物可以是任何食品，从麦当劳的开心乐园餐，到冰淇淋，再到酥脆土豆圈。首先需要决定究竟什么是真正的致肥食品，而且这些食品是否是基本必需品。以牛奶为例。在美国或英国等国家，有多种牛奶可供选择，从脱脂到半脱脂再到全脂。因此，问题就变成了："我们是应该提高这种基本必需品的价格，还是应该专注于其他产品？"在我看来，因为要考虑到底怎么对奶酪或类似的东西进行归类，这可能会使问题更加困难。

先前其他特定食品类型，尤其是糖的价格上涨已经表明，除非价格大幅上涨，且我认为价格翻倍或甚至更多，否则达不到预期效果，而且人们可能会为了购买致肥食品而放弃其他食品。

总之，尽管提高致肥食品的价格是一个好主意，但我认为，要找出哪些食品太"致肥"和应该涨价多少，将是一件棘手的事情。

Task 1

*You should spend about 20 minutes on this task.*

**The maps below show the changes in a school from 1985 to the present day.**

**Summarise the information by selecting and reporting the main features, and make comparisons where relevant.**

*You should write at least 150 words.*

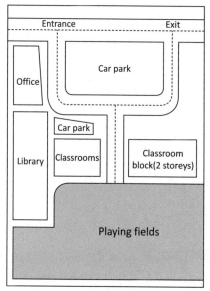

**School in 1985**
**(School population: 1,500 students)**

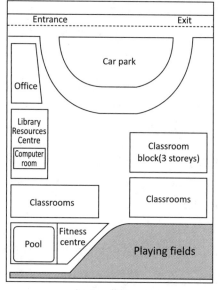

**School now**
**(School population: 2,300 students)**

Task 2

*You should spend about 40 minutes on this task.*

*Write about the following topic:*

**In some countries, online shopping is replacing shopping in stores.**

**Do you think it is a positive or negative development?**

*Give reasons for your answer and include any relevant examples from your own knowledge or experience.*

*You should write at least 250 words.*

Task 1

Two maps are given showing a school back in 1985 facilitating 1,500 students, and the changes to that were made to now cater for 2,300 students.

Looking at the initial map of 1985, the car park is located centrally on the northern side, connected to the southern playing fields. The western side contains an office building above the library. There is a smaller car park above some classrooms, still on the western side of the connecting road. There is a further two-storey classrooms block on the eastern side.

There are considerable differences in the current layout. To begin with, although the location of the main car park remained the same, there is no longer a link to the now much smaller playing field area. The office has been untouched, but the library has been converted into a Learning Resources Centre (LRC) with a computer room. The smaller car park has been demolished, and the western classrooms moved to the south of the LRC where a pool and fitness centre have been added to the southwest corner. The two-storey classroom block is now three storeys, with further new classrooms on its southern side.

In summary, it seems that the playing fields were sacrificed to make room for the changes and that the available classrooms have more than doubled to accommodate the extra 800 students.

***Word Count: 223***

所给的两张地图显示了在 1985 年可容纳 1,500 名学生的一所学校，和它到现在可容纳 2,300 名学生之间所发生的一些变化。

先看第一张 1985 年的地图，停车场位于学校北侧的中心，与学校南侧的运动场相连。学校的西侧在图书馆上方有一座办公楼。在一些教室的上方有一个较小的停车场，仍位于连接道路的西侧。学校东侧还有一栋两层的教室大楼。

现在的布局有相当大的不同。首先，尽管主要停车场的位置保持不变，但不再与现在小得多的运动场区域相连。办公室原封不动，但图书馆被改造成了一个配备计算机室的学习资源中心（LRC）。较小的停车场被拆除，西侧的教室搬到了学习资源中心的南边，在西南角处增加了一个游泳池和一个健身中心。两层的教室大楼现在增高为三层，其南侧还建有更多新教室。

总之，为了给这些变化腾出空间，运动场似乎被舍弃了，可用教室增加了一倍多，以容纳额外的 800 名学生。

Online shopping is now becoming more and more prevalent in countries around the world and is gradually replacing footfall in brick-and-mortar stores. Although many people see this as a positive move into modern times and an inevitable progression, I am not one of them. Many people just see the convenience of online shopping without thinking about the impact of the shift in purchasing methods, namely the elimination of service jobs and income loss for building landlords.

With the growth of shopping apps like TaoBao and JD, many shops in shopping centres have had to close down as they are unable to compete with the prices offered and the shipping capabilities. This means many people have lost their businesses, and the staff have been made redundant without much hope of finding a new position. Taking my local mall as an example, many of the electrical stores have either downsized or simply closed up shop, due to the intense competition from JD.

Another less-known consequence is that with all the in-person shops closing, the mall building owners will also lose income as fewer shops want space. Although some of the retail space has been converted to warehousing and distribution centres for these online platforms, many more have been abandoned and stand empty.

In conclusion, for the lesser-known reasons stated above, I do not believe that the replacement of offline shopping will benefit people in the long run. Offline shopping may have its place, but as a supportive role to the existing shopping routines rather than the elimination of them.

*Word Count: 257*

线上购物现在在世界各国变得越来越普遍，并逐渐取代了实体商店的客流量。尽管许多人认为这是进入当今时代的积极举措，而且是不可避免的进步，但我对此并不同意。许多人仅看到了线上购物的便利，而没有考虑到购买方式的转变所带来的影响，即服务岗位的淘汰和大楼房东的收入损失。

随着淘宝和京东等购物应用程序的发展，许多购物中心的商店不得不关闭，因为它们无法与网购所提供的价格和运输能力相竞争。这意味着许多人失去了他们的生意，员工被裁员，找新工作的希望不大。以我所在的当地商场为例，由于京东的激烈竞争，许多电器商店要么缩小规模，要么关闭商店。

另一个不为人知的后果是，随着所有实体店的关闭，商场建筑的业主也将失去收入，因为需要空间的店铺越来越少。尽管一些零售空间已被改造为这些线上平台的仓储和配送中心，但更多的零售空间已被废弃或闲置。

总之，出于上述较不为人知的原因，从长远来看，我不认为取代线下购物会使人们受益。线下购物可能有它的作用，但是应作为对现有购物习惯的一种支持，而不是淘汰它们。

Task 1

*You should spend about 20 minutes on this task.*

**The diagram gives information about the process of making carbonated drinks.**

**Summarise the information by selecting and reporting on the main features, and make comparisons where relevant.**

*You should write at least 150 words.*

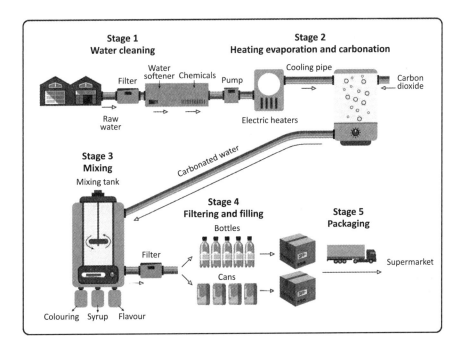

Task 2

*You should spend about 40 minutes on this task.*

*Write about the following topic:*

**People are responsible for their happiness. Others feel happiness depends on other factors in their life.**

**Discuss both views and give your opinion.**

*Give reasons for your answer and include any relevant examples from your own knowledge or experience.*

*You should write at least 250 words.*

Task 1

The diagram given illustrates the process involved in the production of fizzy drinks. It covers five stages, from the delivery of water through to the shipping to the supermarket.

The beginning two stages are concerned with water preparation. Firstly, Raw water is filtered with softener and other chemicals added. It is then pumped into electric heaters to begin stage two. After being heated, the clean water is transported through a cooling pipe into a large container where carbon dioxide is added.

The third stage receives the newly carbonated water into a mixing tank where colouring, syrup and flavour are added and mixed together. The penultimate stage concerns filtering and filling both bottles and cans that are then packed and shipped to a supermarket during the last stage.

In summary, five stages are shown in the process of creating carbonated beverages. However, in the diagram, times for each of the stages are not mentioned.

***Word Count: 153***

所给图表说明了生产碳酸饮料的过程。包括从供水到运输至超市的五个阶段。

开始的两个阶段与水的制备相关。首先，原水通过添加软化剂和其他化学物质进行过滤。之后将原水泵入电加热器，以开始第二阶段。加热后，通过冷却管将净水输送到大容器中，在其中添加二氧化碳。

第三阶段将新碳酸水储存到混合罐中，在其中添加色素、糖浆和香精并将其混合在一起。倒数第二个阶段对瓶罐进行过滤和灌装，之后在最后一个阶段包装并运送到超市。

总之，图中显示了制作碳酸饮料过程中的五个阶段。但并未提及每个阶段所用的时长。

Task 2

Whether people are solely responsible for their happiness or if external factors play a significant role is a complex question. Different individuals may hold varying perspectives on this matter. In this discussion, I will explore both views, and I will provide my opinion.

On the one hand, proponents of the belief that individuals are responsible for their own happiness argue that happiness is an internal state of mind. According to this view, happiness stems from personal attitudes, choices, and perspectives. It suggests that individuals have the ability to cultivate happiness through self-reflection, personal growth, and adopting a positive mindset. Advocates of this viewpoint emphasise the importance of taking responsibility for one's own emotions, finding joy in the present moment, and practising gratitude and mindfulness.

On the other hand, some argue that external factors can significantly impact an individual's happiness. They contend that aspects such as relationships, career satisfaction, financial stability, and physical health substantially influence one's overall well-being. These factors can provide a sense of security, belonging, and purpose, contributing to an individual's happiness. Moreover, societal factors, such as access to education, healthcare, and social support systems, can also shape an individual's happiness level.

I believe the responsibility for one's happiness lies primarily with the individual. Each person has the capacity to develop coping mechanisms, cultivate positive habits, and seek personal fulfilment. However, it is essential to recognise that external factors can significantly impact an individual's happiness. Acknowledging and addressing these external influences, such as improving societal support structures and addressing systemic inequalities, is crucial for promoting overall well-being and happiness on a broader scale.

***Word Count: 265***

　　人的幸福是由自己全权负责，还是外部因素发挥重要作用，这是一个复杂的问题。不同的人可能对这件事有不同的观点。在本次讨论中，我将探讨这两个观点，并提出我的看法。

　　一方面，认为个人需要对其自身幸福负责的拥护者认为，幸福是一种内在的精神状态。根据这一观点，幸福源于个人的态度、选择和观点。这表明，个人有能力通过自我反思、个人成长和采取积极的态度来培养幸福感。这种观点的倡导者强调为自己的情绪负责、在当下寻找快乐、练习感恩和正念的重要性。

　　另一方面，一些人认为外部因素会显著影响个人的幸福感。他们认为，人际关系、职业满意度、财务稳定性和身体健康等方面会极大地影响一个人的整体健康。这些因素可提供安全感、归属感和使命感，均有助于个人幸福。此外，社会因素，例如获得教育、医疗保健和社会支持系统，也可以塑造个人的幸福水平。

　　我认为一个人幸福的责任主要在于个人。每个人均有能力发展应对机制，培养积极的习惯，并寻求个人成就感。然而，重要的是要认识到外部因素会显著影响个人的幸福。承认并解决这些外部影响，例如改善社会支持结构和解决系统性不平等，对于在更广泛的范围内促进整体健康和幸福至关重要。

## ■ Notes and Final Advice from the Author 作者最后的注释和建议

On this last page of the main book, I just wanted to wish everyone who reads it – Good Luck! Any exam can be scary, and certainly when it can potentially have such a profound effect on your future.

在本书的最后一页，我想祝每一位读者——好运！任何考试都可能令人害怕，尤其是可能对你的未来产生深远影响的考试。

Also, remember that the examiners aren't monsters. They're NOT there to try and destroy your life; they're simply there to do a job, and they will do that to the best of their ability. Most examiners I know and have met, above all else, believe in fairness. They truly understand the stakes of the exam and are adverse to the idea of cheating because it's unfair.

另外，记住考官不是怪物。他们不是来摧毁你的生活的，他们只是在恪尽职守，发挥专长。最重要的是，我认识和见过的大多数考官相信公平。他们完全理解考试的利害关系，反对作弊，因为这不公平。

With this in mind, remember there's no shortcut to learning any language. It takes hard work, lots of effort and time. As my mother always said, "You get out what you put in". It means that if you put effort into the learning, you'll be rewarded in kind.

记住这一点，学习任何语言都没有捷径，需要艰苦的工作，付出大量的精力和时间。正如我母亲常说的："你投入什么就会得到什么。"也就是说，只要你努力学习，你就会得到同等的回报。

As a learner of language myself, Chinese in my case, I understand how difficult and frustrating it can be, but I also know how satisfying it can be to learn a new phrase or word you can use in your writing.

作为一名中文学习者，我知道学习一门语言有多么困难和令人沮丧，但我也知道学到一个可以在写作中使用的新的短语或单词有多么满足。

Try not to be too shy, use your English whenever and wherever you can, and try to build your confidence.

不要太害羞，无论何时何地都可以练英语，要自信。

Lastly, as *The Hitchhiker's Guide to the Galaxy* said, "DON'T PANIC!"

最后，站在考场外时，正如《银河系漫游指南》中所说："不要惊慌！"

So, my final piece of advice is BREATHE!

所以，我最后的建议是深呼吸！